PRACTICING TO TAKE THE

GRE®

MATHEMATICS TEST

P9-DEF-333

2nd Edition

INCLUDES:

- An actual GRE Mathematics Test administered in 1992-93
- Sample questions, instructions, and answer sheets
- Percentages of examinees answering each question correctly

AN OFFICIAL PUBLICATION OF THE GRE BOARD

Published by Educational Testing Service
for the Graduate Record Examinations Board

The Graduate Record Examinations Program offers a General Test measuring developed verbal, quantitative, and analytical abilities and Subject Tests measuring achievement in the following 16 fields:

Biochemistry, Cell and Molecular Biology	Economics	Literature in English	Political Science
Biology	Education	Mathematics	Psychology
Chemistry	Engineering	Music	Sociology
Computer Science	Geology	Physics	
	History		

The tests are administered by Educational Testing Service under policies determined by the Graduate Record Examinations Board, an independent board affiliated with the Association of Graduate Schools and the Council of Graduate Schools.

The Graduate Record Examinations Board has officially made available for purchase practice books, each containing a full-length test, for 15 of the Subject Tests. A practice book is not available for the Biochemistry, Cell and Molecular Biology Test at this time. Two General Test practice books are also available.

Individual booklets describing each test and including sample questions are available free of charge for all 16 Subject Tests. You may request these booklets by writing to:

Graduate Record Examinations
Educational Testing Service
P.O. Box 6014
Princeton, NJ 08541-6014

EDUCATIONAL TESTING SERVICE, ETS, the ETS logo, GRADUATE RECORD EXAMINATIONS, and GRE are registered trademarks of Educational Testing Service.

In association with Warner Books, Inc., a Warner Communications Company.

USA: 0-446-39540-4
CAN: 0-446-39541-2

TABLE OF CONTENTS

BACKGROUND FOR THE TEST

TAKING THE TEST

BACKGROUND FOR THE TEST

PRACTICING TO TAKE THE GRE® MATHEMATICS TEST

This practice book has been published on behalf of the Graduate Record Examinations Board to help potential graduate students prepare to take the GRE Mathematics Test. The book contains the actual GRE Mathematics Test administered in February 1993, along with a section of sample questions, and includes information about the purpose of the GRE Subject Tests, a detailed description of the content specifications for the GRE Mathematics Test, and a description of the procedures for developing the test. All test questions that were scored have been included in the practice test.

The sample questions included in this practice book are organized by content category and represent the types of questions included in the test. The purpose of these questions is to provide some indication of the range of topics covered in the test as well as to provide some additional questions for practice purposes. These questions do not represent either the length of the actual test or the proportion of actual test questions within each of the content categories.

Before you take the full-length test, you may want to answer the sample questions. A suggested time limit is provided to give you a rough idea of how much time you would have to complete the sample questions if you were answering them on an actual timed test. After answering the sample questions, evaluate your performance within content categories to determine whether you would benefit by reviewing certain courses.

This practice book contains a complete test book, including the general instructions printed on the back cover. When you take the test at the test center, you will be given time to read these instructions. They show you how to mark your answer sheet properly and give you advice about guessing.

Try to take this practice test under conditions that simulate those in an actual test administration. Use the answer sheets provided on pages 83 to 86 and mark your answers with a No. 2 (soft-lead) pencil as you will do at the test center. Give yourself 2 hours and 50 minutes in a quiet place and work through the test without interruption, focusing your attention on the questions with the same concentration you would use in taking the test to earn a score. Since you will not be permitted to use them at the test center, do not use keyboards, dictionaries or other books, compasses, pamphlets, protractors, highlighter pens, rulers, slide rules, calculators (including watch calculators), stereos or radios with headphones, watch alarms including those with flashing lights or alarm sounds, or paper of any kind.

After you complete the practice test, use the work sheet and conversion tables on pages 25 and 26 to score your test. The work sheet also shows the estimated percent of GRE Mathematics Test examinees from a recent three-year period who answered each question correctly. This will enable you to compare your performance on the questions with theirs. Evaluating your performance on the actual test questions as well as the sample questions should help you determine whether you would benefit further by reviewing certain courses before taking the test at the test center.

We believe that if you use this practice book as we have suggested, you will be able to approach the testing experience with increased confidence.

ADDITIONAL INFORMATION

If you have any questions about any of the information in this book, please write to:

Graduate Record Examinations
Educational Testing Service
P.O. Box 6000
Princeton, NJ 08541-6000

PURPOSE OF THE GRE SUBJECT TESTS

The GRE Subject Tests are designed to help graduate school admission committees and fellowship sponsors assess the qualifications of applicants in their subject fields. The tests also provide students with an assessment of their own qualifications.

Scores on the tests are intended to indicate students' knowledge of the subject matter emphasized in many undergraduate programs as preparation for graduate study. Since past achievement is usually a good indicator of future performance, the scores are helpful in predicting students' success in graduate study. Because the tests are standardized, the test scores permit comparison of students from different institutions with different undergraduate programs.

The Graduate Record Examinations Board recommends that scores on the Subject Tests be considered in conjunction with other relevant information about applicants. Because numerous factors influence success in graduate school, reliance on a single measure to predict success is not advisable. Other indicators of competence typically include undergraduate transcripts showing courses taken and grades earned, letters of recommendation, and GRE General Test scores.

DEVELOPMENT OF THE GRE MATHEMATICS TEST

Each new edition of the Mathematics Test is developed by a committee of examiners composed of professors in the subject who are on undergraduate and graduate faculties in different types of institutions and in different regions of the United States. In selecting members for the committee of examiners, the GRE Program seeks the advice of the Mathematical Association of America.

The content and scope of each test are specified and reviewed periodically by the committee of examiners who, along with other faculty members who are also subject-matter specialists, write the test questions. All questions proposed for the test are reviewed by the committee and revised as necessary. The accepted questions are assembled into a test in accordance with the content specifications developed by the committee of examiners to ensure adequate coverage of the various aspects of the field and at the same time to prevent overemphasis on any single topic. The entire test is then reviewed and approved by the committee.

Subject-matter and measurement specialists on the ETS staff assist the committee of examiners, providing information and advice about methods of test construction and helping to prepare the questions and assemble the test. In addition, they review every test question to identify and eliminate language, symbols, or content considered to be potentially offensive, inappropriate, or serving to perpetuate any negative attitudes. The test as a whole is also reviewed to make sure that the test questions, where applicable, include an appropriate balance of people in different groups and different roles.

Because of the diversity of undergraduate curricula in mathematics, it is not possible for a single test to cover all the material an examinee may have studied.

The examiners, therefore, select questions that test the basic knowledge and understanding most important for successful graduate study in the field. The committee keeps the test up-to-date by regularly developing new editions and revising existing editions. In this way, the test content changes steadily but gradually, much like most curricula.

When a new edition is introduced into the program, it is equated; that is, the scores are related by statistical methods to scores on previous editions so that scores from all editions in use are directly comparable. Although they do not contain the same questions, all editions of the Mathematics Test are constructed according to equivalent specifications for content and level of difficulty, and all measure equivalent knowledge and skills.

After a new edition of the Mathematics Test is first administered, examinees' responses to each test question are analyzed to determine whether the question functioned as expected. This analysis may reveal that a question is ambiguous, requires knowledge beyond the scope of the test, or is inappropriate for the group or a particular subgroup of examinees taking the test. Such questions are not counted in computing examinees' scores.

CONTENT OF THE GRE MATHEMATICS TEST

The test usually consists of 66 multiple-choice questions, some of which may be grouped in sets and based on such materials as diagrams and graphs. The questions are drawn from the courses of study most commonly offered at the undergraduate level. Approximately 50 percent of the questions involve calculus and its applications — subject matter that can be assumed to be common to the backgrounds of almost all mathematics majors. About 25 percent of the questions in the test are in elementary algebra, linear algebra, abstract algebra, and number theory. The remaining portion consists of questions on real and complex analysis as well as questions from several diverse areas of mathematics currently offered to undergraduates in many institutions.

To assist students in preparing for the test, the following content descriptions are presented. The percentages given are approximate; actual percentages will vary slightly from one edition of the test to another.

Calculus (50%)

The usual material of two years of calculus, including trigonometry, coordinate geometry, introductory differential equations, and applications based on the calculus.

Algebra (25%)

Elementary algebra: the kind of algebra taught in precalculus courses

Linear algebra: matrices, linear transformations, characteristic polynomials, eigenvectors, and other standard material

Abstract algebra and number theory: topics from the elementary theory of groups, rings, and fields; elementary topics from number theory

Additional Topics (25%)

Introductory real variable theory as presented in courses, such as those entitled Advanced Calculus or Methods of Real Analysis, that include the elementary topology of the line, plane, 3-space, and n-space, as well as Riemann and elementary Lebesgue integration; other areas such as complex variables, probability and statistics, set theory, logic, combinatorial analysis, general topology, numerical analysis, and algorithmic processes.

There may also be questions that ask the test taker to match "real-life" situations to appropriate mathematical models.

The above descriptions of topics covered in the test should not be considered exhaustive; it is necessary to understand many other related concepts. Knowledge of the material included in the descriptions is a necessary, but not sufficient, condition for correctly answering the questions on the test; and prospective test takers should be aware that a substantial number of questions requiring no more than a good precalculus background are analytically quite complex, and some of these turn out to be among the most difficult questions on the test. In general, the questions are intended to test more than the recall of information and concentrate on assessing the test takers' understanding of fundamental concepts and their ability to apply these concepts in various situations.

SAMPLE QUESTIONS

The sample questions included in this practice book represent the types of questions included in the test. The purpose of the sample questions is to provide some indication of the range of topics covered in the test as well as to provide some additional questions for practice purposes. These questions do not represent either the length of the actual test or the proportion of actual test questions within each of the content categories. A time limit of 140 minutes is suggested to give you a rough idea of how much time you would have to complete the sample questions if you were answering them on an actual timed test. Correct answers to the sample questions are listed on page 22.

<u>Directions</u>: Each of the questions or incomplete statements is followed by five suggested answers or completions. Select the one that is best in each case.

CALCULUS

1. If S is a plane in Euclidean 3-space containing $(0, 0, 0)$, $(2, 0, 0)$, and $(0, 0, 1)$, then S is the

   (A) xy-plane
   (B) xz-plane
   (C) yz-plane
   (D) plane $y - z = 0$
   (E) plane $x + 2y - 2z = 0$

2. $\int_0^1 \int_0^x xy \, dy \, dx =$

   (A) 0   (B) $\frac{1}{8}$ (C) $\frac{1}{3}$ (D) 1   (E) 3

3. For $x \geq 0$, $\frac{d}{dx}(x^e \cdot e^x) =$

   (A) $x^e \cdot e^x + x^{e-1} \cdot e^{x+1}$ (B) $x^e \cdot e^x + x^{e+1} \cdot e^{x-1}$ (C) $x^e \cdot e^x$ (D) $x^{e-1} \cdot e^{x+1}$ (E) $x^{e+1} \cdot e^{x-1}$

4. All functions f defined on the xy-plane such that
   $$\frac{\partial f}{\partial x} = 2x + y \quad \text{and} \quad \frac{\partial f}{\partial y} = x + 2y$$
   are given by $f(x, y) =$

   (A) $x^2 + xy + y^2 + C$ (B) $x^2 - xy + y^2 + C$ (C) $x^2 - xy - y^2 + C$
   (D) $x^2 + 2xy + y^2 + C$ (E) $x^2 - 2xy + y^2 + C$

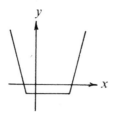

5. Which of the following could be the graph of the derivative of the function whose graph is shown in the figure above?

(A)   (B)   (C)

(D)   (E)

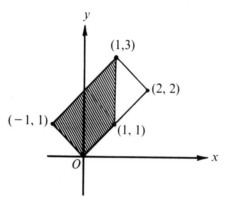

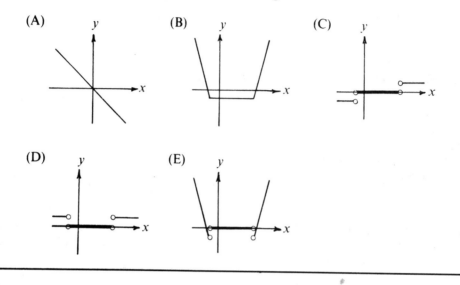

6. Which of the following integrals represents the area of the shaded portion of the rectangle shown in the figure above?

(A) $\int_{-1}^{1} (x + 2 - |x|)\, dx$

(B) $\int_{-1}^{1} (|x| + x + 2)\, dx$

(C) $\int_{-1}^{1} (x + 2)\, dx$

(D) $\int_{-1}^{1} |x|\, dx$

(E) $\int_{-1}^{1} 2\, dx$

7. $\displaystyle\sum_{n=1}^{\infty} \frac{n}{n + 1} =$

(A) $\dfrac{1}{e}$

(B) $\log 2$

(C) 1

(D) e

(E) $+\infty$

8. If $\sin^{-1}x = \frac{\pi}{6}$, then the acute angle value of $\cos^{-1}x$ is

(A) $\frac{5\pi}{6}$ (B) $\frac{\pi}{3}$ (C) $\sqrt{1 - \frac{\pi^2}{6^2}}$ (D) $1 - \frac{\pi}{6}$ (E) 0

9. $\int_0^\pi e^{\sin^2 x} e^{\cos^2 x} dx =$

(A) π (B) $e\pi$ (C) e^π (D) $e^{\sin^2 \pi}$ (E) $e^\pi - 1$

10. Which of the following is true of the behavior of $f(x) = \dfrac{x^3 + 8}{x^2 - 4}$ as $x \to 2$?

(A) The limit is 0.
(B) The limit is 1.
(C) The limit is 4.
(D) The graph of the function has a vertical asymptote at 2.
(E) The function has unequal, finite left-hand and right-hand limits.

11. Suppose that an arrow is shot from a point p and lands at a point q such that at one and only one point in its flight is the arrow parallel to the line of sight between p and q. Of the following, which is the best mathematical model for the phenomenon described above?

(A) A function f differentiable on $[a, b]$ such that there is one and only one point c in $[a, b]$ with
$\int_a^b f'(x)\, dx = c(b - a)$

(B) A function f whose second derivative is at all points negative such that there is one and only one point c in $[a, b]$ with $f'(c) = \dfrac{f(b) - f(a)}{b - a}$

(C) A function f whose first derivative is at all points positive such that there is one and only one point c in $[a, b]$ with $\int_a^b f(x)\, dx = f(c) \cdot (b - a)$

(D) A function f continuous on $[a, b]$ such that there is one and only one point c in $[a, b]$ with
$\int_a^b f(x)\, dx = f(c) \cdot (b - a)$

(E) A function f continuous on $[a, b]$ and $f(a) < d < f(b)$ such that there is one and only one point c in $[a, b]$ with $f(c) = d$

12. If $c > 0$ and $f(x) = e^x - cx$ for all real numbers x, then the minimum value of f is

(A) $f(c)$ (B) $f(e^c)$ (C) $f\left(\frac{1}{c}\right)$ (D) $f(\log c)$ (E) nonexistent

13. For all $x > 0$, if $f(\log x) = \sqrt{x}$, then $f(x) =$

(A) $e^{\frac{x}{2}}$ (B) $\log\sqrt{x}$ (C) $e^{\sqrt{x}}$ (D) $\sqrt{\log x}$ (E) $\dfrac{\log x}{2}$

14. $\int_0^1 \left(\int_0^{\sin y} \frac{1}{\sqrt{1 - x^2}} dx \right) dy =$

   (A) $\frac{1}{3}$ (B) $\frac{1}{2}$ (C) $\frac{\pi}{4}$ (D) 1   (E) $\frac{\pi}{3}$

15. For what triples of real numbers (a, b, c) with $a \neq 0$ is the function

   defined by $f(x) = \begin{cases} x, & \text{if } x \leq 1 \\ ax^2 + bx + c, & \text{if } x > 1 \end{cases}$

   differentiable at all real x ?

   (A) $\{(a, 1 - 2a, a) \mid a$ is a nonzero real number$\}$

   (B) $\{(a, 1 - 2a, c) \mid a, c$ are real numbers and $a \neq 0\}$

   (C) $\{(a, b, c) \mid a, b, c$ are real numbers, $a \neq 0$, and $a + b + c = 1\}$

   (D) $\left\{ \left(\frac{1}{2}, 0, 0 \right) \right\}$

   (E) $\{(a, 1 - 2a, 0) \mid a$ is a nonzero real number$\}$

Questions 16-18 are based on the following information.

   Let f be a function such that the graph of f is a semicircle S with end points $(a, 0)$ and $(b, 0)$ where $a < b$.

16. $\left| \int_a^b f(x) dx \right| =$

   (A) $f(b) - f(a)$ (B) $\frac{f(b) - f(a)}{b - a}$ (C) $(b - a) \frac{\pi}{4}$ (D) $(b - a)^2 \pi$ (E) $(b - a)^2 \frac{\pi}{8}$

17. The graph of $y = 3 f(x)$ is a

   (A) translation of S (B) semicircle with radius three times that of S (C) subset of an ellipse
   (D) subset of a parabola   (E) subset of a hyperbola

18. The improper integral $\int_a^b f(x) f'(x) dx$ is

   (A) necessarily zero
   (B) possibly zero but not necessarily
   (C) necessarily nonexistent
   (D) possibly nonexistent but not necessarily
   (E) none of the above

19. $\lim\limits_{x \to \pi} \frac{e^{-\pi} - e^{-x}}{\sin x} =$

   (A) $-\infty$ (B) $-e^{-\pi}$ (C) 0   (D) $e^{-\pi}$ (E) 1

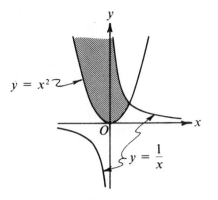

20. The shaded region in the figure above indicates the graph of which of the following?

(A) $x^2 < y$ and $y < \dfrac{1}{x}$

(B) $x^2 < y$ or $y < \dfrac{1}{x}$

(C) $x^2 > y$ and $y > \dfrac{1}{x}$

(D) $x^2 > y$ or $y > \dfrac{1}{x}$

(E) $x^2 < y$ and $xy < 1$

21. The shortest distance from the curve $xy = 8$ to the origin is

(A) 4   (B) 8   (C) 16   (D) $2\sqrt{2}$ (E) $4\sqrt{2}$

22. If $f(x) = \begin{cases} \dfrac{|x|}{x}, & \text{for } x \neq 0 \\ 0, & \text{for } x = 0, \end{cases}$ then $\int_{-1}^{1} f(x)\, dx$ is

(A) -2 (B) 0   (C) 2   (D) not defined

(E) none of the above

23. Let $y = f(x)$ be a solution of the differential equation $x\, dy + (y - xe^x)\, dx = 0$ such that $y = 0$ when $x = 1$. What is the value of $f(2)$?

(A) $\dfrac{1}{2e}$ (B) $\dfrac{1}{e}$ (C) $\dfrac{e^2}{2}$ (D) $2e$ (E) $2e^2$

24. Of the following, which best represents a portion of the graph of $y = \frac{1}{e^x} + x - \frac{1}{e}$ near $(1, 1)$?

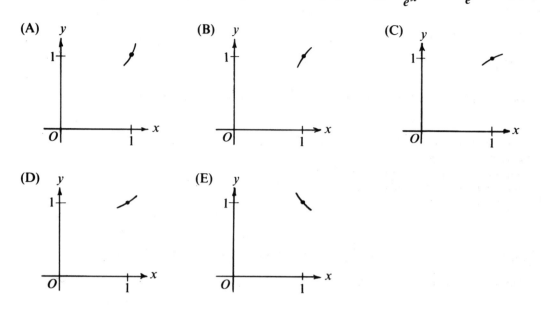

25. In xyz-space, the degree measure of the angle between the rays

$$z = x \geqq 0, \ y = 0$$

and

$$z = y \geqq 0, \ x = 0 \quad \text{is}$$

(A) 0°   (B) 30°   (C) 45°   (D) 60°   (E) 90°

26. Suppose f is a real function such that $f'(x_0)$ exists. Which of the following is the value of

$$\lim_{h \to 0} \frac{f(x_0 + h) - f(x_0 - h)}{h} ?$$

(A) 0   (B) $2f'(x_0)$ (C) $f'(-x_0)$ (D) $-f'(x_0)$ (E) $-2f'(x_0)$

27. The radius of convergence of the series $\displaystyle\sum_{n=0}^{\infty} \frac{e^n}{n!} x^n$ is

(A) 0   (B) $\frac{1}{e}$ (C) 1   (D) e (E) $+\infty$

28. In the xy-plane, the graph of $x^{\log y} = y^{\log x}$ is

(A) empty   (B) a single point   (C) a ray in the open first quadrant

(D) a closed curve   (E) the open first quadrant

14

29. Let $x_1 = 1$ and $x_{n+1} = \sqrt{3 + 2x_n}$ for all positive integers n. If it is assumed that $\{x_n\}$ converges, then
$\lim_{n \to \infty} x_n =$

(A) -1 (B) 0 (C) $\sqrt{5}$ (D) e (E) 3

30. Let $f(x, y) = x^3 + y^3 + 3xy$ for all real x and y. Then there exist distinct points P and Q such that f has a

(A) local maximum at P and at Q
(B) saddle point at P and at Q
(C) local maximum at P and a saddle point at Q
(D) local minimum at P and a saddle point at Q
(E) local minimum at P and at Q

31. The polynomial $p(x) = 1 + \frac{1}{2}(x - 1) - \frac{1}{8}(x - 1)^2$ is used to approximate $\sqrt{1.01}$. Which of the following most closely approximates the error $\sqrt{1.01} - p(1.01)$?

(A) $\left(\frac{1}{16}\right) \times 10^{-6}$ (B) $\left(\frac{1}{48}\right) \times 10^{-8}$ (C) $\left(\frac{3}{8}\right) \times 10^{-10}$

(D) $-\left(\frac{3}{8}\right) \times 10^{-10}$ (E) $-\left(\frac{1}{16}\right) \times 10^{-6}$

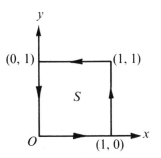

32. If B is the boundary of S as indicated in the figure above, then $\int_B (3y\,dx + 4x\,dy) =$

(A) 0 (B) 1 (C) 3 (D) 4 (E) 7

33. Let f be a continuous, strictly decreasing, real-valued function such that $\int_0^{+\infty} f(x)\,dx$ is finite and $f(0) = 1$. In terms of f^{-1} (the inverse function of f), $\int_0^{+\infty} f(x)\,dx$ is

(A) less than $\int_1^{+\infty} f^{-1}(y)\,dy$ (B) greater than $\int_0^1 f^{-1}(y)\,dy$ (C) equal to $\int_1^{+\infty} f^{-1}(y)\,dy$

(D) equal to $\int_0^1 f^{-1}(y)\,dy$ (E) equal to $\int_0^{+\infty} f^{-1}(y)\,dy$

34. Which of the following indicates the graphs of two functions that satisfy the differential equation

$$\left(\frac{dy}{dx}\right)^2 + 2y\frac{dy}{dx} + y^2 = 0 ?$$

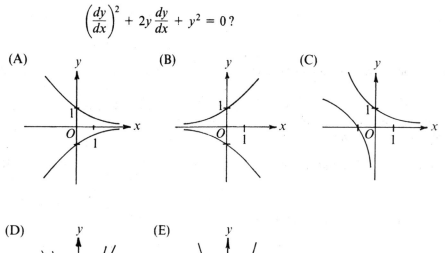

(A)   (B)   (C)

(D)   (E)

ALGEBRA

35. If a, b, and c are real numbers, which of the following are necessarily true?

   I.   If $a < b$ and $ab \neq 0$, then $\frac{1}{a} > \frac{1}{b}$.

   II.   If $a < b$, then $ac < bc$ for all c.

   III.   If $a < b$, then $a + c < b + c$ for all c.

   IV.   If $a < b$, then $-a > -b$.

(A) I only   (B) I and III only   (C) III and IV only   (D) II, III, and IV only   (E) I, II, III, and IV

36. In order to send an undetected message to an agent in the field, each letter in the message is replaced by the number of its position in the alphabet and that number is entered in a matrix M. Thus, for example, "DEAD" becomes the matrix $M = \begin{pmatrix} 4 & 5 \\ 1 & 4 \end{pmatrix}$. In order to further avoid detection, each message with four letters is sent to the agent encoded as MC, where $C = \begin{pmatrix} 2 & -1 \\ 1 & 1 \end{pmatrix}$. If the agent receives the matrix $\begin{pmatrix} 51 & -3 \\ 31 & -8 \end{pmatrix}$, then the message is

(A) RUSH   (B) COME   (C) ROME   (D) CALL

(E) not uniquely determined by the information given

37. If f is a linear transformation from the plane to the real numbers and if $f(1, 1) = 1$ and $f(-1, 0) = 2$, then $f(3, 5) =$

(A) -6 (B) -5 (C) 0   (D) 8   (E) 9

38. Let $*$ be the binary operation on the rational numbers given by $a * b = a + b + 2ab$. Which of the following are true?

   I. $*$ is commutative.
   II. There is a rational number that is a $*$-identity.
   III. Every rational number has a $*$-inverse.

(A) I only   (B) II only   (C) I and II only   (D) I and III only   (E) I, II, and III

39. A group G in which $(ab)^2 = a^2b^2$ for all a, b in G is necessarily

(A) finite
(B) cyclic
(C) of order two
(D) abelian
(E) none of the above

40. Suppose that $f(1 + x) = f(x)$ for all real x. If f is a polynomial and $f(5) = 11$, then $f\left(\frac{15}{2}\right)$ is

(A) -11 (B) 0   (C) 11   (D) $\frac{33}{2}$

(E) not uniquely determined by the information given

41. Let x and y be positive integers such that $3x + 7y$ is divisible by 11. Which of the following must also be divisible by 11 ?

(A) $4x + 6y$ (B) $x + y + 5$ (C) $9x + 4y$ (D) $4x - 9y$ (E) $x + y - 1$

42. The dimension of the subspace spanned by the real vectors

$$\begin{pmatrix} 1 \\ 1 \\ 0 \\ 0 \end{pmatrix}, \begin{pmatrix} 2 \\ 2 \\ 0 \\ 0 \end{pmatrix}, \begin{pmatrix} 0 \\ 1 \\ 0 \\ 0 \end{pmatrix}, \begin{pmatrix} 2 \\ 0 \\ 0 \\ 3 \end{pmatrix}, \begin{pmatrix} 1 \\ -2 \\ 0 \\ 8 \end{pmatrix}, \begin{pmatrix} 0 \\ 0 \\ 0 \\ 0 \end{pmatrix} \quad \text{is}$$

(A) 2   (B) 3   (C) 4   (D) 5   (E) 6

43. The rank of the matrix

$$\begin{pmatrix} 1 & 2 & 3 & 4 & 5 \\ 6 & 7 & 8 & 9 & 10 \\ 11 & 12 & 13 & 14 & 15 \\ 16 & 17 & 18 & 19 & 20 \\ 21 & 22 & 23 & 24 & 25 \end{pmatrix} \quad \text{is}$$

(A) 1   (B) 2   (C) 3   (D) 4   (E) 5

44. If M is the matrix $\begin{pmatrix} 0 & 1 & 0 \\ 0 & 0 & 1 \\ 1 & 0 & 0 \end{pmatrix}$, then M^{100} is

(A) $\begin{pmatrix} 0 & 1 & 0 \\ 0 & 0 & 1 \\ 1 & 0 & 0 \end{pmatrix}$
(B) $\begin{pmatrix} 0 & 0 & 1 \\ 1 & 0 & 0 \\ 0 & 1 & 0 \end{pmatrix}$
(C) $\begin{pmatrix} 1 & 0 & 0 \\ 0 & 1 & 0 \\ 0 & 0 & 1 \end{pmatrix}$
(D) $\begin{pmatrix} 0 & 0 & 0 \\ 0 & 0 & 0 \\ 0 & 0 & 0 \end{pmatrix}$

(E) none of the above

45. If a polynomial $f(x)$ over the real numbers has the complex numbers $2 + i$ and $1 - i$ as roots, then $f(x)$ could be

(A) $x^4 + 6x^3 + 10$
(B) $x^4 + 7x^2 + 10$
(C) $x^3 - x^2 + 4x + 1$
(D) $x^3 + 5x^2 + 4x + 1$
(E) $x^4 - 6x^3 + 15x^2 - 18x + 10$

46. Let V be the set of all real polynomials $p(x)$. Let transformations T, S be defined on V by
$T: p(x) \to xp(x)$ and $S: p(x) \to p'(x) = \frac{d}{dx}p(x)$, and interpret $(ST)(p(x))$ as $S(T(p(x)))$.
Which of the following is true?

(A) $ST = 0$
(B) $ST = T$
(C) $ST = TS$
(D) $ST - TS$ is the identity map of V onto itself.
(E) $ST + TS$ is the identity map of V onto itself.

47. If the finite group G contains a subgroup of order seven but no element (other than the identity) is its own inverse, then the order of G could be

(A) 27   (B) 28   (C) 35   (D) 37   (E) 42

48. Which of the following is the larger of the eigenvalues (characteristic values) of the matrix $\begin{pmatrix} 5 & 1 \\ 1 & 5 \end{pmatrix}$?

(A) 4   (B) 5   (C) 6   (D) 10   (E) 12

49. Let V be the vector space, under the usual operations, of real polynomials that are of degree at most 3. Let W be the subspace of all polynomials $p(x)$ in V such that $p(0) = p(1) = p(-1) = 0$. Then $\dim V + \dim W$ is

(A) 4   (B) 5   (C) 6   (D) 7   (E) 8

50. The map $x \to axa^2$ of a group G into itself is a homomorphism if and only if

(A) G is abelian   (B) $G = \{e\}$ (C) $a = e$ (D) $a^2 = a$ (E) $a^3 = e$

51. Let $I \neq A \neq -I$, where I is the identity matrix and A is a real 2×2 matrix. If $A = A^{-1}$, then the trace of A is

(A) 2   (B) 1   (C) 0   (D) -1 (E) -2

52. Which of the following subsets are subrings of the ring of real numbers?

   I. $\{a + b\sqrt{2}\,|\,a$ and b are rational$\}$

   II. $\left\{\dfrac{n}{3^m}\,|\,n$ is an integer and m is a non-negative integer$\right\}$

   III. $\{a + b\sqrt{5}\,|\,a$ and b are real numbers and $a^2 + b^2 \leq 1\}$

(A) I only   (B) I and II only   (C) I and III only   (D) II and III only   (E) I, II, and III

ADDITIONAL TOPICS

53. k digits are to be chosen at random (with repetitions allowed) from $\{0, 1, 2, 3, 4, 5, 6, 7, 8, 9\}$. What is the probability that 0 will <u>not</u> be chosen?

(A) $\dfrac{1}{k}$ (B) $\dfrac{1}{10}$ (C) $\dfrac{k-1}{k}$ (D) $\left(\dfrac{1}{10}\right)^k$ (E) $\left(\dfrac{9}{10}\right)^k$

54. $S(n)$ is a statement about positive integers n such that whenever $S(k)$ is true, $S(k + 1)$ must also be true. Furthermore, there exists some positive integer n_0 such that $S(n_0)$ is not true. Of the following, which is the strongest conclusion that can be drawn?

(A) $S(n_0 + 1)$ is not true.
(B) $S(n_0 - 1)$ is not true.
(C) $S(n)$ is not true for any $n \leq n_0$.
(D) $S(n)$ is not true for any $n \geq n_0$.
(E) $S(n)$ is not true for any n.

55. Let f and g be functions defined on the positive integers and related in the following way:

$$f(n) = \begin{cases} 1, & \text{if } n = 1 \\ 2f(n - 1), & \text{if } n \neq 1 \end{cases}$$

and

$$g(n) = \begin{cases} 3g(n + 1), & \text{if } n \neq 3 \\ f(n), & \text{if } n = 3. \end{cases}$$

The value of $g(1)$ is

(A) 6   (B) 9   (C) 12   (D) 36

(E) not uniquely determined by the information given

56. If k is a real number and

$$f(x) = \begin{cases} \sin \dfrac{1}{x} & \text{for } x \neq 0 \\ k & \text{for } x = 0 \end{cases}$$

and if the graph of f is <u>not</u> a connected subset of the plane, then the value of k

(A) could be -1
(B) must be 0
(C) must be 1
(D) could be less than 1 and greater than -1
(E) must be less than -1 or greater than 1

57. What is wrong with the following argument?

Let R be the real numbers.

(1) "For all x, $y \in R$, $f(x) + f(y) = f(xy)$."

is equivalent to

(2) "For all x, $y \in R$, $f(-x) + f(y) = f((-x)y)$."

which is equivalent to

(3) "For all x, $y \in R$, $f(-x) + f(y) = f((-x)y) = f(x(-y)) = f(x) + f(-y)$."

From this for $y = 0$, we make the conclusion

(4) "For all $x \in R$, $f(-x) = f(x)$."

Since the steps are reversible, any function with property (4) has property (1).
Therefore, for all x, $y \in R$, $\cos x + \cos y = \cos(xy)$.

(A) (2) does not imply (1).   (B) (3) does not imply (2).   (C) (3) does not imply (4).

(D) (4) does not imply (3).   (E) (4) is not true for $f = \cos$.

58. Suppose that the space S contains exactly eight points. If $\mathcal{G}$ is a collection of 250 distinct subsets of S, which of the following statements must be true?

(A) S is an element of $\mathcal{G}$.

(B) $\bigcap\limits_{G \in \mathcal{G}} G = S$

(C) $\bigcap\limits_{G \in \mathcal{G}} G$ is a nonempty proper subset of S.

(D) $\mathcal{G}$ has a member that contains exactly one element.

(E) The empty set is an element of $\mathcal{G}$.

20

59. In a game two players take turns tossing a fair coin; the winner is the first one to toss a head. The probability that the player who makes the first toss wins the game is

(A) $\frac{1}{4}$ (B) $\frac{1}{3}$ (C) $\frac{1}{2}$ (D) $\frac{2}{3}$ (E) $\frac{3}{4}$

60. Acceptable input for a certain pocket calculator is a finite sequence of characters each of which is either a digit or a sign. The first character must be a digit, the last character must be a digit, and any character that is a sign must be followed by a digit. There are 10 possible digits and 4 possible signs. If N_k denotes the number of such acceptable sequences having length k, then N_k is given recursively by

(A) $N_1 = 10$
    $N_k = 10N_{k-1}$

(B) $N_1 = 10$
    $N_k = 14N_{k-1}$

(C) $N_1 = 10$
    $N_2 = 100$
    $N_k = 10N_{k-1} + 40N_{k-2}$

(D) $N_1 = 10$
    $N_2 = 140$
    $N_k = 14N_{k-1} + 40N_{k-2}$

(E) $N_1 = 14$
    $N_2 = 196$
    $N_k = 10N_{k-1} + 14N_{k-2}$

61. If $f(z)$ is an analytic function that maps the entire finite complex plane into the real axis, then the imaginary axis must be mapped onto

(A) the entire real axis
(B) a point
(C) a ray
(D) an open finite interval
(E) the empty set

62. A fair die is tossed 360 times. The probability that a six comes up on 70 or more of the tosses is

(A) greater than 0.50
(B) between 0.16 and 0.50
(C) between 0.02 and 0.16
(D) between 0.01 and 0.02
(E) less than 0.01

63. Let S be a compact topological space, let T be a topological space, and let f be a function from S onto T. Of the following conditions on f, which is the weakest condition sufficient to ensure the compactness of T?

(A) f is a homeomorphism.
(B) f is continuous and $1-1$.
(C) f is continuous.
(D) f is $1-1$.
(E) f is bounded.

ANSWER KEY FOR SAMPLE QUESTIONS

Calculus

1. B		18. A	
2. B		19. B	
3. A		20. E	
4. A		21. A	
5. C		22. B	
6. A		23. C	
7. E		24. D	
8. B		25. D	
9. B		26. B	
10. D		27. E	
11. B		28. E	
12. D		29. E	
13. A		30. C	
14. B		31. A	
15. A		32. B	
16. E		33. D	
17. C		34. A	

Algebra

	Additional Topics	
35. C	53. E	
36. C	54. C	
37. E	55. D	
38. C	56. E	
39. D	57. D	
40. C	58. D	
41. D	59. D	
42. B	60. C	
43. B	61. B	
44. A	62. C	
45. E	63. C	
46. D		
47. C		
48. C		
49. B		
50. E		
51. C		
52. B		

TAKING THE TEST
TEST-TAKING STRATEGY

Presumably, if you are about to take the GRE Mathematics Test, you are nearing completion of or have completed an undergraduate curriculum in that subject. A general review of your curriculum is probably the best preparation for taking the test. Because the level of difficulty of the test is set to provide reliable measurement over a broad range of subject matter, you are not expected to be able to answer every question correctly.

You are strongly urged to work through some of the sample questions preceding this section. After you have evaluated your performance within the content categories, you may determine that a review of certain courses would be to your benefit.

In preparing to take the full-length Mathematics Test, it is important that you become thoroughly familiar with the directions provided in the full-length test included in this book. For this test, your score will be determined by subtracting one-fourth the number of incorrect answers from the number of correct answers. Questions for which you mark no answer or more than one answer are not counted in scoring. If you have some knowledge of a question and are able to rule out one or more of the answer choices as incorrect, your chances of selecting the correct answer are improved, and answering such questions is likely to improve your score. It is unlikely that pure guessing will raise your score; it may lower your score.

Work as rapidly as you can without being careless. *This includes checking frequently to make sure you are marking your answers in the appropriate rows on your answer sheet.* Since no question carries greater weight than any other, do not waste time pondering individual questions you find extremely difficult or unfamiliar.

You may find it advantageous to go through the test a first time quite rapidly, stopping only to answer those questions of which you are confident. Then go back and answer the questions that require greater thought, concluding with the very difficult questions, if you have time.

HOW TO SCORE YOUR TEST

Total Subject Test scores are reported as three-digit scaled scores with the third digit always zero. The maximum possible range for all Subject Test total scores is from 200 to 990. The actual range of scores for a particular Subject Test, however, may be smaller. Mathematics Test scores typically range from 400 to 990. The range for different editions of a given test may vary because different editions are not of precisely the same difficulty. The differences in ranges among different editions of a given test, however, usually are small. This should be taken into account, especially when comparing two very high scores. In general, differences between scores at the 99th percentile should be ignored. **The score conversions table provided shows the score range for this edition of the test only.**

The work sheet on page 25 lists the correct answers to the questions. Columns are provided for you to mark whether you chose the correct (C) answer or an incorrect (I) answer to each question. Draw a line across any question you omitted, because it is not counted in the scoring. At the bottom of the page, enter the total number correct and the total number incorrect. Divide the total incorrect by 4 and subtract the resulting number from the total correct. This is the adjustment made for guessing. Then round the result to the nearest whole number. This will give you your raw total score. Use the total score conversion table to find the scaled total score that corresponds to your raw total score.

Example: Suppose you chose the correct answers to 48 questions and incorrect answers to 15. Dividing 15 by 4 yields 3.75. Subtracting 3.75 from 48 equals 44.25, which is rounded to 44. The raw score of 44 corresponds to a scaled score of 870.

QUESTION Number	Answer	P +	TOTAL C	I		QUESTION Number	Answer	P +	TOTAL C	I
1	D	96				36	D	68		
2	C	90				37	B	61		
3	A	82				38	D	24		
4	C	71				39	D	62		
5	A	65				40	A	26		
6	B	78				41	B	71		
7	D	72				42	D	22		
8	B	65				43	E	19		
9	E	70				44	D	33		
10	A	89				45	C	46		
11	C	76				46	E	74		
12	E	67				47	C	17		
13	A	56				48	D	53		
14	D	52				49	D	29		
15	D	53				50	A	36		
16	A	61				51	B	29		
17	E	68				52	D	65		
18	D	44				53	A	43		
19	A	54				54	C	54		
20	B	43				55	E	18		
21	D	77				56	B	15		
22	E	69				57	C	56		
23	C	52				58	C	64		
24	A	45				59	A	45		
25	D	33				60	D	15		
26	C	65				61	C	47		
27	A	51				62	B	11		
28	B	40				63	D	41		
29	E	61				64	C	37		
30	E	51				65	A	53		
31	C	59				66	B	44		
32	B	27								
33	C	84								
34	E	57								
35	B	36								

Correct (C) _____

Incorrect (I) _____

Total Score:

C – I/4 = _____

Scaled Score (SS) = _____

*The P+ column indicates the percent of Mathematics Test examinees who answered each question correctly; it is based on a sample of February 1993 examinees selected to represent all Mathematics Test examinees tested between October 1, 1989, and September 30, 1992.

Score Conversions and Percents Below*
for GRE Mathematics Test, Form GR9367

TOTAL SCORE					
Raw Score	Scaled Score	%	Raw Score	Scaled Score	%
55-66	990	91			
54	980	90	26	690	42
53	970	89	25	680	39
52	960	88	24	670	38
51	950	86	23	660	36
50	930	84	22	650	34
49	920	83	21	640	32
48	910	81	20	630	30
47	900	80	19	620	28
			18	600	25
46	890	78			
45	880	77	17	590	23
44	870	75	16	580	21
43	860	74	15	570	19
42	850	72	14	560	17
41	840	70	13	550	16
40	830	69	12	540	14
39	820	67	11	530	12
38	810	65	10	520	11
37	800	63	9	510	10
			8	500	8
36	790	62			
35	780	60	7	490	7
34	770	58	6	480	6
33	760	55	5	470	5
32	750	54	4	460	4
31	740	51	3	450	3
30	730	50	2	440	3
29	720	48	1	430	2
28	710	46	0	420	1
27	700	44			

*Percent scoring below the scaled score is based on the performance of 12,094 examinees who took the Mathematics Test between October 1, 1989, and September 30, 1992. This percent below information was used for score reports during the 1993-94 testing year.

EVALUATING YOUR PERFORMANCE (GR9367)

Now that you have scored your test, you may wish to compare your performance with the performance of others who took this test. Two kinds of information are provided, both using performance data from GRE mathematics examinees tested between October 1989 and September 1992. Interpretive data based on the scores earned by examinees tested in this three-year period are to be used by admissions officers in 1993-94.

The first kind of information is based on the performance of a sample of the examinees who took the test in February 1993. This sample was selected to represent the total population of GRE mathematics examinees tested between October 1989 and September 1992. On the work sheet you used to determine your score is a column labeled "P+." The numbers in this column indicate the percent of the examinees in this sample who answered each question correctly. You may use these numbers as a guide for evaluating your performance on each test question.

Also included, for each scaled score, is the percent of examinees tested between October 1989 and September 1992 who received lower scores. These percents appear in the score conversions table in a column to the right of the scaled scores. For example, in the percent column opposite the scaled score of 870 is the percent 75. This means that 75 percent of the Mathematics Test examinees tested between October 1989 and September 1992 scored lower than 870. To compare yourself with this population, look at the percent next to the scaled score you earned on the practice test. This number is a reasonable indication of your rank among GRE Mathematics Test examinees if you followed the test-taking suggestions in this practice book.

It is important to realize that the conditions under which you tested yourself were not exactly the same as those you will encounter at a test center. It is impossible to predict how different test-taking conditions will affect test performance, and this is only one factor that may account for differences between your practice test scores and your actual test scores. By comparing your performance on this practice test with the performance of other GRE Mathematics Test examinees, however, you will be able to determine your strengths and weaknesses and can then plan a program of study to prepare yourself for taking the Mathematics Test under standard conditions.

Before you start timing yourself on the test that follows, we suggest that you remove an answer sheet (pages 83 to 86) and turn first to the back cover of the test book (page 81), as you will do at the test center, and follow the instructions for completing the identification areas of the answer sheet. When you are ready to begin the test, note the time and start marking your answers to the questions on the answer sheet.

THE GRADUATE RECORD
EXAMINATIONS®

GRE®

Ⓔ🅃Ⓢ®

MATHEMATICS TEST

Do not break the seal
until you are told to do so.

The contents of this test are confidential.
Disclosure or reproduction of any portion
of it is prohibited.

THIS TEST BOOK MUST NOT BE TAKEN FROM THE ROOM.

MATHEMATICS TEST

Time—170 minutes

66 Questions

Directions: Each of the questions or incomplete statements below is followed by five suggested answers or completions. In each case, select the one that is the best of the choices offered and then mark the corresponding space on the answer sheet.

Computation and scratchwork may be done in this examination book.

Note: In this examination:

(1) All logarithms are to the base e unless otherwise specified.
(2) The set of all x such that $a \le x \le b$ is denoted by $[a, b]$.

1. If $f(g(x)) = 5$ and $f(x) = x + 3$ for all real x, then $g(x) =$

(A) $x - 3$ (B) $3 - x$ (C) $\dfrac{5}{x + 3}$ (D) 2   (E) 8

2. $\lim\limits_{x \to 0} \dfrac{\tan x}{\cos x} =$

(A) $-\infty$ (B) -1 (C) 0   (D) 1   (E) $+\infty$

3. $\displaystyle\int_0^{\log 4} e^{2x}dx =$

(A) $\dfrac{15}{2}$ (B) 8   (C) $\dfrac{17}{2}$ (D) $\dfrac{\log 16}{2} - 1$ (E) $\log 4 - \dfrac{1}{2}$

4. Let $A - B$ denote $\{x \in A : x \notin B\}$. If $(A - B) \cup B = A$, which of the following must be true?

(A) B is empty.
(B) $A \subseteq B$
(C) $B \subseteq A$
(D) $(B - A) \cup A = B$
(E) None of the above

GO ON TO THE NEXT PAGE.

SCRATCHWORK

5. If $f(x) = |x| + 3x^2$ for all real x, then $f'(-1)$ is

(A) -7 (B) -5 (C) 5 (D) 7 (E) nonexistent

---

6. For what value of b is the value of $\int_b^{b+1} (x^2 + x)\, dx$ a minimum?

(A) 0 (B) -1 (C) -2 (D) -3 (E) -4

---

7. In how many of the eight standard octants of xyz-space does the graph of $z = e^{x+y}$ appear?

(A) One   (B) Two   (C) Three   (D) Four   (E) Eight

---

8. Suppose that the function f is defined on an interval by the formula $f(x) = \sqrt{\tan^2 x - 1}$. If f is continuous, which of the following intervals could be its domain?

(A) $\left(\dfrac{3\pi}{4}, \pi \right)$

(B) $\left(\dfrac{\pi}{4}, \dfrac{\pi}{2} \right)$

(C) $\left(\dfrac{\pi}{4}, \dfrac{3\pi}{4} \right)$

(D) $\left(-\dfrac{\pi}{4}, 0 \right)$

(E) $\left(-\dfrac{3\pi}{4}, -\dfrac{\pi}{4} \right)$

GO ON TO THE NEXT PAGE.

SCRATCHWORK

9. $\displaystyle\int_0^1 \frac{x}{2-x^2}\,dx =$

  (A) $-\dfrac{1}{2}$ (B) $\dfrac{5}{3}$ (C) $\dfrac{\log 2 - e}{2}$ (D) $-\dfrac{\log 2}{2}$ (E) $\dfrac{\log 2}{2}$

---

10. If $f''(x) = f'(x)$ for all real x, and if $f(0) = 0$ and $f'(0) = -1$, then $f(x) =$

  (A) $1 - e^x$ (B) $e^x - 1$ (C) $e^{-x} - 1$ (D) e^{-x} (E) $-e^x$

---

11. If $\phi(x, y, z) = x^2 + 2xy + xz^{\frac{3}{2}}$, which of the following partial derivatives are identically zero?

  I. $\dfrac{\partial^2 \phi}{\partial y^2}$

  II. $\dfrac{\partial^2 \phi}{\partial x \partial y}$

  III. $\dfrac{\partial^2 \phi}{\partial z \partial y}$

  (A) III only
  (B) I and II only
  (C) I and III only
  (D) II and III only
  (E) I, II, and III

GO ON TO THE NEXT PAGE.

12. $\displaystyle\lim_{x \to 0} \frac{\sin 2x}{(1 + x)\log(1 + x)} =$

(A) -2 (B) $-\dfrac{1}{2}$ (C) 0 (D) $\dfrac{1}{2}$ (E) 2

---

13. $\displaystyle\lim_{n \to \infty} \int_1^n \frac{1}{x^n} \, dx =$

(A) 0 (B) 1 (C) e (D) π (E) $+\infty$

---

14. At a 15 percent annual inflation rate, the value of the dollar would decrease by approximately one-half every 5 years. At this inflation rate, in approximately how many years would the dollar be worth $\dfrac{1}{1,000,000}$ of its present value?

(A) 25   (B) 50   (C) 75   (D) 100   (E) 125

GO ON TO THE NEXT PAGE.

15. Let $f(x) = \int_1^x \dfrac{1}{1 + t^2}\, dt$ for all real x. An equation of the line tangent to the graph of f at the point $(2, f(2))$ is

(A) $y - 1 = \dfrac{1}{5}(x - 2)$ (B) $y - \text{Arctan } 2 = \dfrac{1}{5}(x - 2)$ (C) $y - 1 = (\text{Arctan } 2)(x - 2)$

(D) $y - \text{Arctan } 2 + \dfrac{\pi}{4} = \dfrac{1}{5}(x - 2)$ (E) $y - \dfrac{\pi}{2} = (\text{Arctan } 2)(x - 2)$

---

16. Let $f(x) = e^{g(x)}h(x)$ and $h'(x) = -g'(x)h(x)$ for all real x. Which of the following must be true?

(A) f is a constant function.
(B) f is a linear nonconstant function.
(C) g is a constant function.
(D) g is a linear nonconstant function.
(E) None of the above

---

17. $1 - \sin^2\left(\text{Arccos } \dfrac{\pi}{12}\right) =$

(A) $\sqrt{\dfrac{1 - \cos \dfrac{\pi}{24}}{2}}$ (B) $\sqrt{\dfrac{1 - \cos \dfrac{\pi}{6}}{2}}$ (C) $\sqrt{\dfrac{1 + \cos \dfrac{\pi}{24}}{2}}$ (D) $\dfrac{\pi}{6}$ (E) $\dfrac{\pi^2}{144}$

GO ON TO THE NEXT PAGE.

SCRATCHWORK

18. If $f(x) = \sum_{n=0}^{\infty} (-1)^n x^{2n}$ for all $x \in (0, 1)$, then $f'(x) =$

(A) $\sin\ x$ 　　　(B) $\cos\ x$ 　　　(C) $\dfrac{1}{1 + x^2}$ 　　　(D) $\dfrac{-2x}{(1 + x^2)^2}$ 　　　(E) $\dfrac{2x}{(1 - 2x)^2}$

19. Which of the following is the general solution of the differential equation

$$\frac{d^3y}{dt^3} - 3\frac{d^2y}{dt^2} + 3\frac{dy}{dt} - y = 0\ ?$$

(A) $c_1 e^t + c_2 t e^t + c_3 t^2 e^t$

(B) $c_1 e^{-t} + c_2 t e^{-t} + c_3 t^2 e^{-t}$

(C) $c_1 e^t - c_2 e^{-t} + c_3 t e^{t^2}$

(D) $c_1 e^t + c_2 e^{2t} + c_3 e^{3t}$

(E) $c_1 e^{2t} + c_2 t e^{-2t}$

GO ON TO THE NEXT PAGE.

20. Which of the following double integrals represents the volume of the solid bounded above by the graph of $z = 6 - x^2 - 2y^2$ and bounded below by the graph of $z = -2 + x^2 + 2y^2$?

(A) $4\int_{x=0}^{x=2} \int_{y=0}^{y=\sqrt{2}} (8 - 2x^2 - 4y^2)\ dy\ dx$

(B) $\int_{x=-2}^{x=2} \int_{y=-\sqrt{(4 - x^2)/2}}^{y=\sqrt{(4 - x^2)/2}} (8 - 2x^2 - 4y^2)\ dy\ dx$

(C) $4\int_{y=0}^{y=\sqrt{2}} \int_{x=-\sqrt{4 - 2y^2}}^{x=\sqrt{4 - 2y^2}} dx\ dy$

(D) $\int_{y=-\sqrt{2}}^{y=\sqrt{2}} \int_{x=-2}^{x=2} (8 - 2x^2 - 4y^2)\ dx\ dy$

(E) $2\int_{y=0}^{y=\sqrt{2}} \int_{x=0}^{x=\sqrt{4 - 2y^2}} (8 - 2x^2 - 4y^2)\ dx\ dy$

___

21. Let a be a number in the interval $[0, 1]$ and let f be a function defined on $[0, 1]$ by

$$f(x) = \begin{cases} a^2 & \text{if } 0 \le x \le a, \\ ax & \text{otherwise.} \end{cases}$$

Then the value of a for which $\int_0^1 f(x)\ dx = 1$ is

(A) $\frac{1}{4}$ (B) $\frac{1}{3}$ (C) $\frac{1}{2}$ (D) 1   (E) nonexistent

___

GO ON TO THE NEXT PAGE.

SCRATCHWORK

22. If b and c are elements in a group G, and if $b^5 = c^3 = e$, where e is the unit element of G, then the inverse of $b^2cb^4c^2$ must be

(A) b^3c^2bc (B) $b^4c^2b^2c$ (C) $c^2b^4cb^2$ (D) $cb^2c^2b^4$ (E) cbc^2b^3

---

23. Let f be a real-valued function continuous on the closed interval $[0, 1]$ and differentiable on the open interval $(0, 1)$ with $f(0) = 1$ and $f(1) = 0$. Which of the following must be true?

   I. There exists $x \in (0, 1)$ such that $f(x) = x$.
   II. There exists $x \in (0, 1)$ such that $f'(x) = -1$.
   III. $f(x) > 0$ for all $x \in [0, 1)$.

(A) I only   (B) II only   (C) I and II only   (D) II and III only   (E) I, II, and III

---

24. If A and B are events in a probability space such that $0 < P(A) = P(B) = P(A \cap B) < 1$, which of the following CANNOT be true?

(A) A and B are independent.   (B) A is a proper subset of B.   (C) $A \neq B$

(D) $A \cap B = A \cup B$ (E) $P(A)P(B) < P(A \cap B)$

GO ON TO THE NEXT PAGE.

25. Let f be a real-valued function with domain $[0, 1]$. If there is some $K > 0$ such that $f(x) - f(y) \le K|x - y|$ for all x and y in $[0, 1]$, which of the following must be true?

(A) f is discontinuous at each point of $(0, 1)$.
(B) f is not continuous on $(0, 1)$, but is discontinuous at only countably many points of $(0, 1)$.
(C) f is continuous on $(0, 1)$, but is differentiable at only countably many points of $(0, 1)$.
(D) f is continuous on $(0, 1)$, but may not be differentiable on $(0, 1)$.
(E) f is differentiable on $(0, 1)$.

26. Let $\mathbf{i} = (1, 0, 0)$, $\mathbf{j} = (0, 1, 0)$, and $\mathbf{k} = (0, 0, 1)$. The vectors $\mathbf{v}_1$ and $\mathbf{v}_2$ are orthogonal if $\mathbf{v}_1 = \mathbf{i} + \mathbf{j} - \mathbf{k}$ and $\mathbf{v}_2 =$

(A) $\mathbf{i} + \mathbf{j} - \mathbf{k}$ (B) $\mathbf{i} - \mathbf{j} + \mathbf{k}$ (C) $\mathbf{i} + \mathbf{k}$ (D) $\mathbf{j} - \mathbf{k}$ (E) $\mathbf{i} + \mathbf{j}$

27. If the curve in the yz-plane with equation $z = f(y)$ is rotated around the y-axis, an equation of the resulting surface of revolution is

(A) $x^2 + z^2 = [f(y)]^2$
(B) $x^2 + z^2 = f(y)$
(C) $x^2 + z^2 = |f(y)|$
(D) $y^2 + z^2 = |f(y)|$
(E) $y^2 + z^2 = [f(x)]^2$

GO ON TO THE NEXT PAGE.

28. Let A and B be subspaces of a vector space V. Which of the following must be subspaces of V?

    I. $A + B = \{a + b: \; a \in A \text{ and } b \in B\}$
    II. $A \cup B$
    III. $A \cap B$
    IV. $\{x \in V: \; x \notin A\}$

    (A) I and II only
    (B) I and III only
    (C) III and IV only
    (D) I, II, and III only
    (E) I, II, III, and IV

---

29. $\displaystyle \lim_{n \to \infty} \sum_{k=1}^{n} \left(\frac{1}{k} - \frac{1}{2^k} \right) =$

    (A) 0   (B) 1   (C) 2   (D) 4   (E) $+\infty$

---

30. If $f(x_1, \ldots, x_n) = \displaystyle\sum_{1 \le i < j \le n} x_i x_j$, then $\dfrac{\partial f}{\partial x_n} =$

    (A) $n!$ (B) $\displaystyle\sum_{1 \le i < j < n} x_i x_j$ (C) $\displaystyle\sum_{1 \le i < j < n} (x_i + x_j)$ (D) $\displaystyle\sum_{j=1}^{n} x_j$ (E) $\displaystyle\sum_{j=1}^{n-1} x_j$

GO ON TO THE NEXT PAGE.

31. If $f(x) = \begin{cases} \sqrt{1 - x^2} & \text{for } 0 \le x \le 1 \\ x - 1 & \text{for } 1 < x \le 2, \end{cases}$

then $\int_0^2 f(x)\,dx$ is

(A) $\dfrac{\pi}{2}$

(B) $\dfrac{\sqrt{2}}{2}$

(C) $\dfrac{1}{2} + \dfrac{\pi}{4}$

(D) $\dfrac{1}{2} + \dfrac{\pi}{2}$

(E) undefined

---

32. Let R denote the field of real numbers, Q the field of rational numbers, and Z the ring of integers. Which of the following subsets F_i of R, $1 \le i \le 4$, are subfields of R?

$$F_1 = \{a/b:\ a, b \in Z \text{ and } b \text{ is odd}\}$$
$$F_2 = \{a + b\sqrt{2}:\ a, b \in Z\}$$
$$F_3 = \{a + b\sqrt{2}:\ a, b \in Q\}$$
$$F_4 = \{a + b\sqrt[4]{2}:\ a, b \in Q\}$$

(A) No F_i is a subfield of R.

(B) F_3 only

(C) F_2 and F_3 only

(D) F_1, F_2, and F_3 only

(E) F_1, F_2, F_3, and F_4

GO ON TO THE NEXT PAGE.

SCRATCHWORK

33. If n apples, no two of the same weight, are lined up at random on a table, what is the probability that they are lined up in order of increasing weight from left to right?

(A) $\dfrac{1}{2}$ (B) $\dfrac{1}{n}$ (C) $\dfrac{1}{n!}$ (D) $\dfrac{1}{2^n}$ (E) $\left(\dfrac{1}{n}\right)^n$

34. $\dfrac{d}{dx} \displaystyle\int_0^{x^2} e^{-t^2}\, dt =$

(A) e^{-x^2} (B) $2e^{-x^2}$ (C) $2e^{-x^4}$ (D) $x^2 e^{-x^2}$ (E) $2x e^{-x^4}$

GO ON TO THE NEXT PAGE.

SCRATCHWORK

35. Let f be a real-valued function defined on the set of integers and satisfying $f(x) = \frac{1}{2}f(x - 1) + \frac{1}{2}f(x + 1)$. Which of the following must be true?

    I. The graph of f is a subset of a line.
    II. f is strictly increasing.
    III. f is a constant function.

(A) None
(B) I only
(C) II only
(D) I and II
(E) I and III

---

36. If F is a function such that, for all positive integers x and y, $F(x, 1) = x + 1$, $F(1, y) = 2y$, and $F(x + 1, y + 1) = F(F(x, y + 1), y)$, then $F(2, 2) =$

(A) 8   (B) 7   (C) 6   (D) 5   (E) 4

---

37. If $\det \begin{pmatrix} a & b & c \\ d & e & f \\ g & h & k \end{pmatrix} = 9$, then $\det \begin{pmatrix} 3a & 3b & 3c \\ g-4a & h-4b & k-4c \\ d & e & f \end{pmatrix} =$

(A) -108 (B) -27 (C) 3   (D) 12   (E) 27

GO ON TO THE NEXT PAGE.

SCRATCHWORK

38. $\lim\limits_{n\to\infty} \dfrac{3}{n}\sum\limits_{i=1}^{n}\left[\left(\dfrac{3i}{n}\right)^2 - \left(\dfrac{3i}{n}\right)\right] =$

(A) $-\dfrac{1}{6}$ (B) 0 (C) 3 (D) $\dfrac{9}{2}$ (E) $\dfrac{31}{6}$

39. For a real number x, $\log(1 + \sin 2\pi x)$ is <u>not</u> a real number if and only if x is

(A) an integer

(B) nonpositive

(C) equal to $\dfrac{2n - 1}{2}$ for some integer n

(D) equal to $\dfrac{4n - 1}{4}$ for some integer n

(E) any real number

40. If x, y, and z are selected independently and at random from the interval $[0, 1]$, then the probability that $x \geq yz$ is

(A) $\dfrac{3}{4}$ (B) $\dfrac{2}{3}$ (C) $\dfrac{1}{2}$ (D) $\dfrac{1}{3}$ (E) $\dfrac{1}{4}$

GO ON TO THE NEXT PAGE.

41. If $A = \begin{pmatrix} 1 & 2 \\ 0 & -1 \end{pmatrix}$, then the set of all vectors X for which $AX = X$ is

(A) $\left\{ \begin{pmatrix} a \\ b \end{pmatrix} \middle| a = 0 \text{ and } b \text{ is arbitrary} \right\}$

(B) $\left\{ \begin{pmatrix} a \\ b \end{pmatrix} \middle| a \text{ is arbitrary and } b = 0 \right\}$

(C) $\left\{ \begin{pmatrix} a \\ b \end{pmatrix} \middle| a = -b \text{ and } b \text{ is arbitrary} \right\}$

(D) $\left\{ \begin{pmatrix} 0 \\ 0 \end{pmatrix} \right\}$

(E) the empty set

---

42. What is the greatest value of b for which any real-valued function f that satisfies the following properties must also satisfy $f(1) < 5$?

(i) f is infinitely differentiable on the real numbers;
(ii) $f(0) = 1$, $f'(0) = 1$, and $f''(0) = 2$; and
(iii) $|f'''(x)| < b$ for all x in $[0, 1]$.

(A) 1   (B) 2   (C) 6   (D) 12   (E) 24

GO ON TO THE NEXT PAGE.

43. Let n be an integer greater than 1. Which of the following conditions guarantee that the equation

$$x^n = \sum_{i=0}^{n-1} a_i x^i \text{ has at least one root in the interval } (0, 1)?$$

   I. $a_0 > 0$ and $\displaystyle\sum_{i=0}^{n-1} a_i < 1$

   II. $a_0 > 0$ and $\displaystyle\sum_{i=0}^{n-1} a_i > 1$

   III. $a_0 < 0$ and $\displaystyle\sum_{i=0}^{n-1} a_i > 1$

(A) None
(B) I only
(C) II only
(D) III only
(E) I and III

---

44. If x is a real number and P is a polynomial function, then $\displaystyle\lim_{h \to 0} \frac{P(x + 3h) + P(x - 3h) - 2P(x)}{h^2} =$

(A) 0   (B) $6P'(x)$ (C) $3P''(x)$ (D) $9P''(x)$ (E) ∞

GO ON TO THE NEXT PAGE.

45. Consider the system of equations

$$ax^2 + by^3 = c$$
$$dx^2 + ey^3 = f$$

where a, b, c, d, e, and f are real constants and $ae \neq bd$. The maximum possible number of real solutions (x, y) of the system is

(A) none (B) one (C) two (D) three (E) five

46. If $x^3 - x + 1 = a_0 + a_1(x - 2) + a_2(x - 2)^2 + a_3(x - 2)^3$ for all real numbers x, then (a_0, a_1, a_2, a_3) is

(A) $\left(1, \frac{1}{2}, 0, -\frac{1}{8}\right)$

(B) $(1, -1, 0, 1)$

(C) $(7, 6, 10, 1)$

(D) $(7, 11, 12, 6)$

(E) $(7, 11, 6, 1)$

GO ON TO THE NEXT PAGE.

SCRATCHWORK

47. Let C be the ellipse with center $(0, 0)$, major axis of length $2a$, and minor axis of length $2b$. The value of $\oint_C x\,dy - y\,dx$ is

(A) $\pi\sqrt{a^2 + b^2}$

(B) $2\pi\sqrt{a^2 + b^2}$

(C) $2\pi ab$

(D) πab

(E) $\dfrac{\pi ab}{2}$

---

48. Let G_n denote the cyclic group of order n. Which of the following direct products is NOT cyclic?

(A) $G_{17} \times G_{11}$

(B) $G_{17} \times G_{11} \times G_5$

(C) $G_{17} \times G_{33}$

(D) $G_{22} \times G_{33}$

(E) $G_{49} \times G_{121}$

GO ON TO THE NEXT PAGE.

SCRATCHWORK

49. Let X be a random variable with probability density function

$$f(x) = \begin{cases} \dfrac{3}{4}(1 - x^2) & \text{if } -1 \le x \le 1, \\ 0 & \text{otherwise.} \end{cases}$$

What is the standard deviation of X?

(A) 0 (B) $\dfrac{1}{5}$ (C) $\dfrac{\sqrt{30}}{15}$ (D) $\dfrac{1}{\sqrt{5}}$ (E) 1

---

50. The set of all points (x, y, z) in Euclidean 3-space such that

$$\begin{vmatrix} 1 & x & y & z \\ 1 & 1 & 0 & 0 \\ 1 & 0 & 1 & 0 \\ 1 & 0 & 0 & 1 \end{vmatrix} = 0$$

is

(A) a plane containing the points $(1, 0, 0)$, $(0, 1, 0)$, and $(0, 0, 1)$
(B) a sphere with center at the origin and radius 1
(C) a surface containing the point $(1, 1, 1)$
(D) a vector space with basis $\{(1, 0, 0), (0, 1, 0), (0, 0, 1)\}$
(E) none of the above

GO ON TO THE NEXT PAGE.

SCRATCHWORK

51. An automorphism ϕ of a field F is a one-to-one mapping of F onto itself such that $\phi(a + b) = \phi(a) + \phi(b)$ and $\phi(ab) = \phi(a)\phi(b)$ for all $a, b \in F$. If F is the field of rational numbers, then the number of distinct automorphisms of F is

(A) 0 (B) 1 (C) 2 (D) 4 (E) infinite

52. Let T be the transformation of the xy-plane that reflects each vector through the x-axis and then doubles the vector's length.

If A is the 2×2 matrix such that $T\left(\begin{bmatrix} x \\ y \end{bmatrix}\right) = A\begin{bmatrix} x \\ y \end{bmatrix}$ for each vector $\begin{bmatrix} x \\ y \end{bmatrix}$, then $A =$

(A) $\begin{bmatrix} 0 & 2 \\ 2 & 0 \end{bmatrix}$

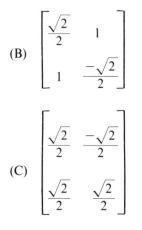

(B) $\begin{bmatrix} \dfrac{\sqrt{2}}{2} & 1 \\ 1 & \dfrac{-\sqrt{2}}{2} \end{bmatrix}$

(C) $\begin{bmatrix} \dfrac{\sqrt{2}}{2} & \dfrac{-\sqrt{2}}{2} \\ \dfrac{\sqrt{2}}{2} & \dfrac{\sqrt{2}}{2} \end{bmatrix}$

(D) $\begin{bmatrix} 2 & 0 \\ 0 & -2 \end{bmatrix}$

(E) $\begin{bmatrix} 0 & -2 \\ -2 & 0 \end{bmatrix}$

GO ON TO THE NEXT PAGE.

SCRATCHWORK

53. Let $r > 0$ and let C be the circle $|z| = r$ in the complex plane. If P is a polynomial function, then $\int_C P(z)\, dz =$

(A) 0
(B) πr^2
(C) $2\pi i$
(D) $2\pi P(0)i$
(E) $P(r)$

---

54. If f and g are real-valued differentiable functions and if $f'(x) \geq g'(x)$ for all x in the closed interval $[0, 1]$, which of the following must be true?

(A) $f(0) \geq g(0)$

(B) $f(1) \geq g(1)$

(C) $f(1) - g(1) \geq f(0) - g(0)$

(D) $f - g$ has no maximum on $[0, 1]$.

(E) $\dfrac{f}{g}$ is a nondecreasing function on $[0, 1]$.

---

55. Let p and q be distinct primes. There is a proper subgroup J of the additive group of integers which contains exactly three elements of the set $\{p, p + q, pq, p^q, q^p\}$. Which three elements are in J?

(A) pq, p^q, q^p
(B) $p + q, pq, p^q$
(C) $p, p + q, pq$
(D) p, p^q, q^p
(E) p, pq, p^q

GO ON TO THE NEXT PAGE.

SCRATCHWORK

56. For a subset S of a topological space X, let $cl(S)$ denote the closure of S in X, and let $S' = \{x: x \in cl(S - \{x\})\}$ denote the derived set of S. If A and B are subsets of X, which of the following statements are true?

  I. $(A \cup B)' = A' \cup B'$
  II. $(A \cap B)' = A' \cap B'$
  III. If A' is empty, then A is closed in X.
  IV. If A is open in X, then A' is not empty.

  (A) I and II only
  (B) I and III only
  (C) II and IV only
  (D) I, II, and III only
  (E) I, II, III, and IV

57. Consider the following procedure for determining whether a given name appears in an alphabetized list of n names.

  Step 1. Choose the name at the middle of the list (if $n = 2k$, choose the kth name); if that is the given name, you are done; if the list is only one name long, you are done. If you are not done, go to Step 2.

  Step 2. If the given name comes alphabetically before the name at the middle of the list, apply Step 1 to the first half of the list; otherwise, apply Step 1 to the second half of the list.

  If n is very large, the maximum number of steps required by this procedure is close to

  (A) n

  (B) n^2

  (C) $\log_2 n$

  (D) $n \log_2 n$

  (E) $n^2 \log_2 n$

GO ON TO THE NEXT PAGE.

SCRATCHWORK

58. Which of the following is an eigenvalue of the matrix

$$\begin{pmatrix} 2 & 1 - i \\ 1 + i & -2 \end{pmatrix}$$

over the complex numbers?

(A) 0   (B) 1   (C) $\sqrt{6}$ (D) i (E) $1 + i$

---

59. Two subgroups H and K of a group G have orders 12 and 30, respectively. Which of the following could NOT be the order of the subgroup of G generated by H and K?

(A) 30   (B) 60   (C) 120   (D) 360   (E) Countable infinity

---

60. Let A and B be subsets of a set M and let $S_0 = \{A, B\}$. For $i \geq 0$, define S_{i+1} inductively to be the collection of subsets X of M that are of the form $C \cup D$, $C \cap D$, or $M - C$ (the complement of C in M), where $C, D \in S_i$. Let $S = \bigcup_{i=0}^{\infty} S_i$. What is the largest possible number of elements of S?

(A) 4
(B) 8
(C) 15
(D) 16
(E) S may be infinite.

GO ON TO THE NEXT PAGE.

SCRATCHWORK

61. A city has square city blocks formed by a grid of north-south and east-west streets. One automobile route from City Hall to the main firehouse is to go exactly 5 blocks east and 7 blocks north. How many different routes from City Hall to the main firehouse traverse exactly 12 city blocks?

(A) $5 \cdot 7$

(B) $\dfrac{7!}{5!}$

(C) $\dfrac{12!}{7!5!}$

(D) 2^{12}

(E) $7!5!$

---

62. Let R be the set of real numbers with the topology generated by the basis $\{[a, b): a < b,$ where $a, b \in R\}$. If X is the subset $[0, 1]$ of R, which of the following must be true?

   I. X is compact.
  II. X is Hausdorff.
 III. X is connected.

(A) I only
(B) II only
(C) III only
(D) I and II
(E) II and III

GO ON TO THE NEXT PAGE.

SCRATCHWORK

63. Let R be the circular region of the xy-plane with center at the origin and radius 2.
Then $\int_R\int e^{-(x^2 + y^2)}dx\, dy =$

(A) 4π

(B) πe^{-4}

(C) $4\pi e^{-4}$

(D) $\pi(1 - e^{-4})$

(E) $4\pi(e - e^{-4})$

64. Let V be the real vector space of real-valued functions defined on the real numbers and having derivatives of all orders. If D is the mapping from V into V that maps every function in V to its derivative, what are all the eigenvectors of D?

(A) All nonzero functions in V

(B) All nonzero constant functions in V

(C) All nonzero functions of the form $ke^{\lambda x}$, where k and λ are real numbers

(D) All nonzero functions of the form $\displaystyle\sum_{i=0}^{k} c_i x^i$, where $k > 0$ and the c_i's are real numbers

(E) There are no eigenvectors of D.

GO ON TO THE NEXT PAGE.

65. If f is a function defined by a complex power series expansion in $z - a$ which converges for $|z - a| < 1$ and diverges for $|z - a| > 1$, which of the following must be true?

(A) $f(z)$ is analytic in the open unit disk with center at a.

(B) The power series for $f(z + a)$ converges for $|z + a| < 1$.

(C) $f'(a) = 0$

(D) $\int_C f(z)dz = 0$ for any circle C in the plane.

(E) $f(z)$ has a pole of order 1 at $z = a$.

66. Let n be any positive integer and $1 \leq x_1 < x_2 < \ldots < x_{n+1} \leq 2n$, where each x_i is an integer. Which of the following must be true?

    I. There is an x_i that is the square of an integer.
   II. There is an i such that $x_{i+1} = x_i + 1$.
  III. There is an x_i that is prime.

(A) I only
(B) II only
(C) I and II
(D) I and III
(E) II and III

IF YOU FINISH BEFORE TIME IS CALLED, YOU MAY CHECK YOUR WORK ON THIS TEST.

NOTE: To ensure prompt processing of test results, it is important that you fill in the blanks exactly as directed.

SUBJECT TEST

A. Print and sign your full name in this box:

PRINT: _____
        (LAST)   (FIRST)   (MIDDLE)

SIGN: _____

Copy this code in box 6 on your answer sheet. Then fill in the corresponding ovals exactly as shown.

6. TITLE CODE

6 7 6 1 0

Copy the Test Name and Form Code in box 7 on your answer sheet.

TEST NAME _____Mathematics_____

FORM CODE _____GR 9367_____

GRADUATE RECORD EXAMINATIONS SUBJECT TEST

3. The Subject Tests are intended to measure your achievement in a specialized field of study. Most of the questions are concerned with subject matter that is probably familiar to you, but some of the questions may refer to areas that you have not studied.

Your score will be determined by subtracting one-fourth the number of incorrect answers from the number of correct answers. Questions for which you mark no answer or more than one answer are not counted in scoring. If you have some knowledge of a question and are able to rule out one or more of the answer choices as incorrect, your chances of selecting the correct answer are improved, and answering such questions will likely improve your score. It is unlikely that pure guessing will raise your score; it may lower your score.

You are advised to use your time effectively and to work as rapidly as you can without losing accuracy. Do not spend too much time on questions that are too difficult for you. Go on to the other questions and come back to the difficult ones later if you can.

YOU MUST INDICATE ALL YOUR ANSWERS ON THE SEPARATE ANSWER SHEET. No credit will be given for anything written in this examination book, but you may write in the book as much as you wish to work out your answers. After you have decided on your response to a question, fill in the corresponding oval on the answer sheet. BE SURE THAT EACH MARK IS DARK AND COMPLETELY FILLS THE OVAL. Mark only one answer to each question. No credit will be given for multiple answers. Erase all stray marks. If you change an answer, be sure that all previous marks are erased completely. Incomplete erasures may be read as intended answers. Do not be concerned that the answer sheet provides spaces for more answers than there are questions in the test.

Example:

What city is the capital of France?

(A) Rome
(B) Paris
(C) London
(D) Cairo
(E) Oslo

Sample Answer

Ⓐ ● Ⓒ Ⓓ Ⓔ   CORRECT ANSWER PROPERLY MARKED

Ⓐ Ⓑ Ⓒ Ⓓ Ⓔ
Ⓐ Ⓑ Ⓒ Ⓓ Ⓔ
Ⓐ Ⓑ Ⓒ Ⓓ Ⓔ   IMPROPER MARKS
Ⓐ Ⓑ Ⓒ Ⓓ Ⓔ

DO NOT OPEN YOUR TEST BOOK UNTIL YOU ARE TOLD TO DO SO.

DO NOT USE INK

Use only a pencil with soft, black lead (No. 2 or HB) to complete this answer sheet.
Be sure to fill in completely the space that corresponds to your answer choice.
Completely erase any errors or stray marks.

1. NAME

Last Name only (Family or Surname) - first 15 letters

Enter your last name, first name initial (given name), and middle initial if you have one.
Omit spaces, apostrophes, Jr., II., etc.

First Name Initial

Middle Initial

2.

YOUR NAME:
(Print)
Last Name (Family or Surname)   First Name (Given)   M.I.

MAILING ADDRESS:
(Print)
P.O. Box or Street Address

City

Country

State or Province

Zip or Postal Code

CENTER:
City

Country

Center Number

State or Province

Room Number

3. DATE OF BIRTH

Month	Day	Year
Jan.		
Feb.		
Mar.		
April		
May		
June		
July		
Aug.		
Sept.		
Oct.		
Nov.		
Dec.		

4. SOCIAL SECURITY NUMBER
(U.S.A. only)

5. REGISTRATION NUMBER
(from your admission ticket)

6. TITLE CODE
(on back cover of your test book)

7. TEST NAME (on back cover of your test book)

FORM CODE (on back cover of your test book)

8. TEST BOOK SERIAL NUMBER
(red number in upper right corner of front cover of your test book)

SHADED AREA FOR ETS USE ONLY

BE SURE EACH MARK IS DARK AND COMPLETELY FILLS THE INTENDED SPACE AS ILLUSTRATED HERE: ●
YOU MAY FIND MORE RESPONSE SPACES THAN YOU NEED. IF SO, PLEASE LEAVE THEM BLANK.

1 Ⓐ Ⓑ Ⓒ Ⓓ Ⓔ	39 Ⓐ Ⓑ Ⓒ Ⓓ Ⓔ	77 Ⓐ Ⓑ Ⓒ Ⓓ Ⓔ
2 Ⓐ Ⓑ Ⓒ Ⓓ Ⓔ	40 Ⓐ Ⓑ Ⓒ Ⓓ Ⓔ	78 Ⓐ Ⓑ Ⓒ Ⓓ Ⓔ
3 Ⓐ Ⓑ Ⓒ Ⓓ Ⓔ	41 Ⓐ Ⓑ Ⓒ Ⓓ Ⓔ	79 Ⓐ Ⓑ Ⓒ Ⓓ Ⓔ
4 Ⓐ Ⓑ Ⓒ Ⓓ Ⓔ	42 Ⓐ Ⓑ Ⓒ Ⓓ Ⓔ	80 Ⓐ Ⓑ Ⓒ Ⓓ Ⓔ
5 Ⓐ Ⓑ Ⓒ Ⓓ Ⓔ	43 Ⓐ Ⓑ Ⓒ Ⓓ Ⓔ	81 Ⓐ Ⓑ Ⓒ Ⓓ Ⓔ
6 Ⓐ Ⓑ Ⓒ Ⓓ Ⓔ	44 Ⓐ Ⓑ Ⓒ Ⓓ Ⓔ	82 Ⓐ Ⓑ Ⓒ Ⓓ Ⓔ
7 Ⓐ Ⓑ Ⓒ Ⓓ Ⓔ	45 Ⓐ Ⓑ Ⓒ Ⓓ Ⓔ	83 Ⓐ Ⓑ Ⓒ Ⓓ Ⓔ
8 Ⓐ Ⓑ Ⓒ Ⓓ Ⓔ	46 Ⓐ Ⓑ Ⓒ Ⓓ Ⓔ	84 Ⓐ Ⓑ Ⓒ Ⓓ Ⓔ
9 Ⓐ Ⓑ Ⓒ Ⓓ Ⓔ	47 Ⓐ Ⓑ Ⓒ Ⓓ Ⓔ	85 Ⓐ Ⓑ Ⓒ Ⓓ Ⓔ
10 Ⓐ Ⓑ Ⓒ Ⓓ Ⓔ	48 Ⓐ Ⓑ Ⓒ Ⓓ Ⓔ	86 Ⓐ Ⓑ Ⓒ Ⓓ Ⓔ
11 Ⓐ Ⓑ Ⓒ Ⓓ Ⓔ	49 Ⓐ Ⓑ Ⓒ Ⓓ Ⓔ	87 Ⓐ Ⓑ Ⓒ Ⓓ Ⓔ
12 Ⓐ Ⓑ Ⓒ Ⓓ Ⓔ	50 Ⓐ Ⓑ Ⓒ Ⓓ Ⓔ	88 Ⓐ Ⓑ Ⓒ Ⓓ Ⓔ
13 Ⓐ Ⓑ Ⓒ Ⓓ Ⓔ	51 Ⓐ Ⓑ Ⓒ Ⓓ Ⓔ	89 Ⓐ Ⓑ Ⓒ Ⓓ Ⓔ
14 Ⓐ Ⓑ Ⓒ Ⓓ Ⓔ	52 Ⓐ Ⓑ Ⓒ Ⓓ Ⓔ	90 Ⓐ Ⓑ Ⓒ Ⓓ Ⓔ
15 Ⓐ Ⓑ Ⓒ Ⓓ Ⓔ	53 Ⓐ Ⓑ Ⓒ Ⓓ Ⓔ	91 Ⓐ Ⓑ Ⓒ Ⓓ Ⓔ
16 Ⓐ Ⓑ Ⓒ Ⓓ Ⓔ	54 Ⓐ Ⓑ Ⓒ Ⓓ Ⓔ	92 Ⓐ Ⓑ Ⓒ Ⓓ Ⓔ
17 Ⓐ Ⓑ Ⓒ Ⓓ Ⓔ	55 Ⓐ Ⓑ Ⓒ Ⓓ Ⓔ	93 Ⓐ Ⓑ Ⓒ Ⓓ Ⓔ
18 Ⓐ Ⓑ Ⓒ Ⓓ Ⓔ	56 Ⓐ Ⓑ Ⓒ Ⓓ Ⓔ	94 Ⓐ Ⓑ Ⓒ Ⓓ Ⓔ
19 Ⓐ Ⓑ Ⓒ Ⓓ Ⓔ	57 Ⓐ Ⓑ Ⓒ Ⓓ Ⓔ	95 Ⓐ Ⓑ Ⓒ Ⓓ Ⓔ
20 Ⓐ Ⓑ Ⓒ Ⓓ Ⓔ	58 Ⓐ Ⓑ Ⓒ Ⓓ Ⓔ	96 Ⓐ Ⓑ Ⓒ Ⓓ Ⓔ
21 Ⓐ Ⓑ Ⓒ Ⓓ Ⓔ	59 Ⓐ Ⓑ Ⓒ Ⓓ Ⓔ	97 Ⓐ Ⓑ Ⓒ Ⓓ Ⓔ
22 Ⓐ Ⓑ Ⓒ Ⓓ Ⓔ	60 Ⓐ Ⓑ Ⓒ Ⓓ Ⓔ	98 Ⓐ Ⓑ Ⓒ Ⓓ Ⓔ
23 Ⓐ Ⓑ Ⓒ Ⓓ Ⓔ	61 Ⓐ Ⓑ Ⓒ Ⓓ Ⓔ	99 Ⓐ Ⓑ Ⓒ Ⓓ Ⓔ
24 Ⓐ Ⓑ Ⓒ Ⓓ Ⓔ	62 Ⓐ Ⓑ Ⓒ Ⓓ Ⓔ	100 Ⓐ Ⓑ Ⓒ Ⓓ Ⓔ
25 Ⓐ Ⓑ Ⓒ Ⓓ Ⓔ	63 Ⓐ Ⓑ Ⓒ Ⓓ Ⓔ	101 Ⓐ Ⓑ Ⓒ Ⓓ Ⓔ
26 Ⓐ Ⓑ Ⓒ Ⓓ Ⓔ	64 Ⓐ Ⓑ Ⓒ Ⓓ Ⓔ	102 Ⓐ Ⓑ Ⓒ Ⓓ Ⓔ
27 Ⓐ Ⓑ Ⓒ Ⓓ Ⓔ	65 Ⓐ Ⓑ Ⓒ Ⓓ Ⓔ	103 Ⓐ Ⓑ Ⓒ Ⓓ Ⓔ
28 Ⓐ Ⓑ Ⓒ Ⓓ Ⓔ	66 Ⓐ Ⓑ Ⓒ Ⓓ Ⓔ	104 Ⓐ Ⓑ Ⓒ Ⓓ Ⓔ
29 Ⓐ Ⓑ Ⓒ Ⓓ Ⓔ	67 Ⓐ Ⓑ Ⓒ Ⓓ Ⓔ	105 Ⓐ Ⓑ Ⓒ Ⓓ Ⓔ
30 Ⓐ Ⓑ Ⓒ Ⓓ Ⓔ	68 Ⓐ Ⓑ Ⓒ Ⓓ Ⓔ	106 Ⓐ Ⓑ Ⓒ Ⓓ Ⓔ
31 Ⓐ Ⓑ Ⓒ Ⓓ Ⓔ	69 Ⓐ Ⓑ Ⓒ Ⓓ Ⓔ	107 Ⓐ Ⓑ Ⓒ Ⓓ Ⓔ
32 Ⓐ Ⓑ Ⓒ Ⓓ Ⓔ	70 Ⓐ Ⓑ Ⓒ Ⓓ Ⓔ	108 Ⓐ Ⓑ Ⓒ Ⓓ Ⓔ
33 Ⓐ Ⓑ Ⓒ Ⓓ Ⓔ	71 Ⓐ Ⓑ Ⓒ Ⓓ Ⓔ	109 Ⓐ Ⓑ Ⓒ Ⓓ Ⓔ
34 Ⓐ Ⓑ Ⓒ Ⓓ Ⓔ	72 Ⓐ Ⓑ Ⓒ Ⓓ Ⓔ	110 Ⓐ Ⓑ Ⓒ Ⓓ Ⓔ
35 Ⓐ Ⓑ Ⓒ Ⓓ Ⓔ	73 Ⓐ Ⓑ Ⓒ Ⓓ Ⓔ	111 Ⓐ Ⓑ Ⓒ Ⓓ Ⓔ
36 Ⓐ Ⓑ Ⓒ Ⓓ Ⓔ	74 Ⓐ Ⓑ Ⓒ Ⓓ Ⓔ	112 Ⓐ Ⓑ Ⓒ Ⓓ Ⓔ
37 Ⓐ Ⓑ Ⓒ Ⓓ Ⓔ	75 Ⓐ Ⓑ Ⓒ Ⓓ Ⓔ	113 Ⓐ Ⓑ Ⓒ Ⓓ Ⓔ
38 Ⓐ Ⓑ Ⓒ Ⓓ Ⓔ	76 Ⓐ Ⓑ Ⓒ Ⓓ Ⓔ	114 Ⓐ Ⓑ Ⓒ Ⓓ Ⓔ

SIDE 2

SUBJECT TEST

COMPLETE THE CERTIFICATION STATEMENT, THEN TURN ANSWER SHEET OVER TO SIDE 1.

BE SURE EACH MARK IS DARK AND COMPLETELY FILLS THE INTENDED SPACE AS ILLUSTRATED HERE: ●.
YOU MAY FIND MORE RESPONSE SPACES THAN YOU NEED. IF SO, PLEASE LEAVE THEM BLANK.

115 Ⓐ Ⓑ Ⓒ Ⓓ Ⓔ   147 Ⓐ Ⓑ Ⓒ Ⓓ Ⓔ   179 Ⓐ Ⓑ Ⓒ Ⓓ Ⓔ   211 Ⓐ Ⓑ Ⓒ Ⓓ Ⓔ
116 Ⓐ Ⓑ Ⓒ Ⓓ Ⓔ   148 Ⓐ Ⓑ Ⓒ Ⓓ Ⓔ   180 Ⓐ Ⓑ Ⓒ Ⓓ Ⓔ   212 Ⓐ Ⓑ Ⓒ Ⓓ Ⓔ
117 Ⓐ Ⓑ Ⓒ Ⓓ Ⓔ   149 Ⓐ Ⓑ Ⓒ Ⓓ Ⓔ   181 Ⓐ Ⓑ Ⓒ Ⓓ Ⓔ   213 Ⓐ Ⓑ Ⓒ Ⓓ Ⓔ
118 Ⓐ Ⓑ Ⓒ Ⓓ Ⓔ   150 Ⓐ Ⓑ Ⓒ Ⓓ Ⓔ   182 Ⓐ Ⓑ Ⓒ Ⓓ Ⓔ   214 Ⓐ Ⓑ Ⓒ Ⓓ Ⓔ
119 Ⓐ Ⓑ Ⓒ Ⓓ Ⓔ   151 Ⓐ Ⓑ Ⓒ Ⓓ Ⓔ   183 Ⓐ Ⓑ Ⓒ Ⓓ Ⓔ   215 Ⓐ Ⓑ Ⓒ Ⓓ Ⓔ
120 Ⓐ Ⓑ Ⓒ Ⓓ Ⓔ   152 Ⓐ Ⓑ Ⓒ Ⓓ Ⓔ   184 Ⓐ Ⓑ Ⓒ Ⓓ Ⓔ   216 Ⓐ Ⓑ Ⓒ Ⓓ Ⓔ
121 Ⓐ Ⓑ Ⓒ Ⓓ Ⓔ   153 Ⓐ Ⓑ Ⓒ Ⓓ Ⓔ   185 Ⓐ Ⓑ Ⓒ Ⓓ Ⓔ   217 Ⓐ Ⓑ Ⓒ Ⓓ Ⓔ
122 Ⓐ Ⓑ Ⓒ Ⓓ Ⓔ   154 Ⓐ Ⓑ Ⓒ Ⓓ Ⓔ   186 Ⓐ Ⓑ Ⓒ Ⓓ Ⓔ   218 Ⓐ Ⓑ Ⓒ Ⓓ Ⓔ
123 Ⓐ Ⓑ Ⓒ Ⓓ Ⓔ   155 Ⓐ Ⓑ Ⓒ Ⓓ Ⓔ   187 Ⓐ Ⓑ Ⓒ Ⓓ Ⓔ   219 Ⓐ Ⓑ Ⓒ Ⓓ Ⓔ
124 Ⓐ Ⓑ Ⓒ Ⓓ Ⓔ   156 Ⓐ Ⓑ Ⓒ Ⓓ Ⓔ   188 Ⓐ Ⓑ Ⓒ Ⓓ Ⓔ   220 Ⓐ Ⓑ Ⓒ Ⓓ Ⓔ
125 Ⓐ Ⓑ Ⓒ Ⓓ Ⓔ   157 Ⓐ Ⓑ Ⓒ Ⓓ Ⓔ   189 Ⓐ Ⓑ Ⓒ Ⓓ Ⓔ   221 Ⓐ Ⓑ Ⓒ Ⓓ Ⓔ
126 Ⓐ Ⓑ Ⓒ Ⓓ Ⓔ   158 Ⓐ Ⓑ Ⓒ Ⓓ Ⓔ   190 Ⓐ Ⓑ Ⓒ Ⓓ Ⓔ   222 Ⓐ Ⓑ Ⓒ Ⓓ Ⓔ
127 Ⓐ Ⓑ Ⓒ Ⓓ Ⓔ   159 Ⓐ Ⓑ Ⓒ Ⓓ Ⓔ   191 Ⓐ Ⓑ Ⓒ Ⓓ Ⓔ   223 Ⓐ Ⓑ Ⓒ Ⓓ Ⓔ
128 Ⓐ Ⓑ Ⓒ Ⓓ Ⓔ   160 Ⓐ Ⓑ Ⓒ Ⓓ Ⓔ   192 Ⓐ Ⓑ Ⓒ Ⓓ Ⓔ   224 Ⓐ Ⓑ Ⓒ Ⓓ Ⓔ
129 Ⓐ Ⓑ Ⓒ Ⓓ Ⓔ   161 Ⓐ Ⓑ Ⓒ Ⓓ Ⓔ   193 Ⓐ Ⓑ Ⓒ Ⓓ Ⓔ   225 Ⓐ Ⓑ Ⓒ Ⓓ Ⓔ
130 Ⓐ Ⓑ Ⓒ Ⓓ Ⓔ   162 Ⓐ Ⓑ Ⓒ Ⓓ Ⓔ   194 Ⓐ Ⓑ Ⓒ Ⓓ Ⓔ   226 Ⓐ Ⓑ Ⓒ Ⓓ Ⓔ
131 Ⓐ Ⓑ Ⓒ Ⓓ Ⓔ   163 Ⓐ Ⓑ Ⓒ Ⓓ Ⓔ   195 Ⓐ Ⓑ Ⓒ Ⓓ Ⓔ   227 Ⓐ Ⓑ Ⓒ Ⓓ Ⓔ
132 Ⓐ Ⓑ Ⓒ Ⓓ Ⓔ   164 Ⓐ Ⓑ Ⓒ Ⓓ Ⓔ   196 Ⓐ Ⓑ Ⓒ Ⓓ Ⓔ   228 Ⓐ Ⓑ Ⓒ Ⓓ Ⓔ
133 Ⓐ Ⓑ Ⓒ Ⓓ Ⓔ   165 Ⓐ Ⓑ Ⓒ Ⓓ Ⓔ   197 Ⓐ Ⓑ Ⓒ Ⓓ Ⓔ   229 Ⓐ Ⓑ Ⓒ Ⓓ Ⓔ
134 Ⓐ Ⓑ Ⓒ Ⓓ Ⓔ   166 Ⓐ Ⓑ Ⓒ Ⓓ Ⓔ   198 Ⓐ Ⓑ Ⓒ Ⓓ Ⓔ   230 Ⓐ Ⓑ Ⓒ Ⓓ Ⓔ
135 Ⓐ Ⓑ Ⓒ Ⓓ Ⓔ   167 Ⓐ Ⓑ Ⓒ Ⓓ Ⓔ   199 Ⓐ Ⓑ Ⓒ Ⓓ Ⓔ   231 Ⓐ Ⓑ Ⓒ Ⓓ Ⓔ
136 Ⓐ Ⓑ Ⓒ Ⓓ Ⓔ   168 Ⓐ Ⓑ Ⓒ Ⓓ Ⓔ   200 Ⓐ Ⓑ Ⓒ Ⓓ Ⓔ   232 Ⓐ Ⓑ Ⓒ Ⓓ Ⓔ
137 Ⓐ Ⓑ Ⓒ Ⓓ Ⓔ   169 Ⓐ Ⓑ Ⓒ Ⓓ Ⓔ   201 Ⓐ Ⓑ Ⓒ Ⓓ Ⓔ   233 Ⓐ Ⓑ Ⓒ Ⓓ Ⓔ
138 Ⓐ Ⓑ Ⓒ Ⓓ Ⓔ   170 Ⓐ Ⓑ Ⓒ Ⓓ Ⓔ   202 Ⓐ Ⓑ Ⓒ Ⓓ Ⓔ   234 Ⓐ Ⓑ Ⓒ Ⓓ Ⓔ
139 Ⓐ Ⓑ Ⓒ Ⓓ Ⓔ   171 Ⓐ Ⓑ Ⓒ Ⓓ Ⓔ   203 Ⓐ Ⓑ Ⓒ Ⓓ Ⓔ   235 Ⓐ Ⓑ Ⓒ Ⓓ Ⓔ
140 Ⓐ Ⓑ Ⓒ Ⓓ Ⓔ   172 Ⓐ Ⓑ Ⓒ Ⓓ Ⓔ   204 Ⓐ Ⓑ Ⓒ Ⓓ Ⓔ   236 Ⓐ Ⓑ Ⓒ Ⓓ Ⓔ
141 Ⓐ Ⓑ Ⓒ Ⓓ Ⓔ   173 Ⓐ Ⓑ Ⓒ Ⓓ Ⓔ   205 Ⓐ Ⓑ Ⓒ Ⓓ Ⓔ   237 Ⓐ Ⓑ Ⓒ Ⓓ Ⓔ
142 Ⓐ Ⓑ Ⓒ Ⓓ Ⓔ   174 Ⓐ Ⓑ Ⓒ Ⓓ Ⓔ   206 Ⓐ Ⓑ Ⓒ Ⓓ Ⓔ   238 Ⓐ Ⓑ Ⓒ Ⓓ Ⓔ
143 Ⓐ Ⓑ Ⓒ Ⓓ Ⓔ   175 Ⓐ Ⓑ Ⓒ Ⓓ Ⓔ   207 Ⓐ Ⓑ Ⓒ Ⓓ Ⓔ   239 Ⓐ Ⓑ Ⓒ Ⓓ Ⓔ
144 Ⓐ Ⓑ Ⓒ Ⓓ Ⓔ   176 Ⓐ Ⓑ Ⓒ Ⓓ Ⓔ   208 Ⓐ Ⓑ Ⓒ Ⓓ Ⓔ   240 Ⓐ Ⓑ Ⓒ Ⓓ Ⓔ
145 Ⓐ Ⓑ Ⓒ Ⓓ Ⓔ   177 Ⓐ Ⓑ Ⓒ Ⓓ Ⓔ   209 Ⓐ Ⓑ Ⓒ Ⓓ Ⓔ   241 Ⓐ Ⓑ Ⓒ Ⓓ Ⓔ
146 Ⓐ Ⓑ Ⓒ Ⓓ Ⓔ   178 Ⓐ Ⓑ Ⓒ Ⓓ Ⓔ   210 Ⓐ Ⓑ Ⓒ Ⓓ Ⓔ   242 Ⓐ Ⓑ Ⓒ Ⓓ Ⓔ

TR	TW	TFS	TCS	1R	1W	1FS	1CS	2R	2W	2FS	2CS
	FOR ETS USE ONLY			3R	3W	3FS	3CS	4R	4W	4FS	4CS
				5R	5W	5FS	5CS	6R	6W	6FS	6CS

DO NOT USE INK

GRADUATE RECORD EXAMINATIONS® - GRE® - SUBJECT TEST

SIDE 1

Use only a pencil with soft, black lead (No. 2 or HB) to complete this answer sheet.

Be sure to fill in completely the space that corresponds to your answer choice.

Completely erase any errors or stray marks.

1. NAME

Enter your last name, first name initial (given name), and middle initial if you have one.

Omit spaces, apostrophes, Jr., II., etc.

Last Name only (Family or Surname) - first 15 letters

First Name Initial

Middle Initial

2. YOUR NAME:

(Print) Last Name (Family or Surname)   First Name (Given)   M.I.

MAILING ADDRESS:
(Print)

P.O. Box or Street Address

City   State or Province

Country   Zip or Postal Code

CENTER:

City   State or Province

Country

Center Number   Room Number

3. DATE OF BIRTH

Month	Day	Year
Jan.		
Feb.		
Mar.		
April		
May		
June		
July		
Aug.		
Sept.		
Oct.		
Nov.		
Dec.		

4. SOCIAL SECURITY NUMBER
(U.S.A. only)

5. REGISTRATION NUMBER
(from your admission ticket)

6. TITLE CODE
(on back cover of your test book)

7. TEST NAME (on back cover of your test book)

FORM CODE (on back cover of your test book)

8. TEST BOOK SERIAL NUMBER
(red number in upper right corner of front cover of your test book)

SHADED AREA FOR ETS USE ONLY

BE SURE EACH MARK IS DARK AND COMPLETELY FILLS THE INTENDED SPACE AS ILLUSTRATED HERE:

YOU MAY FIND MORE RESPONSE SPACES THAN YOU NEED. IF SO, PLEASE LEAVE THEM BLANK.

1 Ⓐ Ⓑ Ⓒ Ⓓ Ⓔ	39 Ⓐ Ⓑ Ⓒ Ⓓ Ⓔ	77 Ⓐ Ⓑ Ⓒ Ⓓ Ⓔ
2 Ⓐ Ⓑ Ⓒ Ⓓ Ⓔ	40 Ⓐ Ⓑ Ⓒ Ⓓ Ⓔ	78 Ⓐ Ⓑ Ⓒ Ⓓ Ⓔ
3 Ⓐ Ⓑ Ⓒ Ⓓ Ⓔ	41 Ⓐ Ⓑ Ⓒ Ⓓ Ⓔ	79 Ⓐ Ⓑ Ⓒ Ⓓ Ⓔ
4 Ⓐ Ⓑ Ⓒ Ⓓ Ⓔ	42 Ⓐ Ⓑ Ⓒ Ⓓ Ⓔ	80 Ⓐ Ⓑ Ⓒ Ⓓ Ⓔ
5 Ⓐ Ⓑ Ⓒ Ⓓ Ⓔ	43 Ⓐ Ⓑ Ⓒ Ⓓ Ⓔ	81 Ⓐ Ⓑ Ⓒ Ⓓ Ⓔ
6 Ⓐ Ⓑ Ⓒ Ⓓ Ⓔ	44 Ⓐ Ⓑ Ⓒ Ⓓ Ⓔ	82 Ⓐ Ⓑ Ⓒ Ⓓ Ⓔ
7 Ⓐ Ⓑ Ⓒ Ⓓ Ⓔ	45 Ⓐ Ⓑ Ⓒ Ⓓ Ⓔ	83 Ⓐ Ⓑ Ⓒ Ⓓ Ⓔ
8 Ⓐ Ⓑ Ⓒ Ⓓ Ⓔ	46 Ⓐ Ⓑ Ⓒ Ⓓ Ⓔ	84 Ⓐ Ⓑ Ⓒ Ⓓ Ⓔ
9 Ⓐ Ⓑ Ⓒ Ⓓ Ⓔ	47 Ⓐ Ⓑ Ⓒ Ⓓ Ⓔ	85 Ⓐ Ⓑ Ⓒ Ⓓ Ⓔ
10 Ⓐ Ⓑ Ⓒ Ⓓ Ⓔ	48 Ⓐ Ⓑ Ⓒ Ⓓ Ⓔ	86 Ⓐ Ⓑ Ⓒ Ⓓ Ⓔ
11 Ⓐ Ⓑ Ⓒ Ⓓ Ⓔ	49 Ⓐ Ⓑ Ⓒ Ⓓ Ⓔ	87 Ⓐ Ⓑ Ⓒ Ⓓ Ⓔ
12 Ⓐ Ⓑ Ⓒ Ⓓ Ⓔ	50 Ⓐ Ⓑ Ⓒ Ⓓ Ⓔ	88 Ⓐ Ⓑ Ⓒ Ⓓ Ⓔ
13 Ⓐ Ⓑ Ⓒ Ⓓ Ⓔ	51 Ⓐ Ⓑ Ⓒ Ⓓ Ⓔ	89 Ⓐ Ⓑ Ⓒ Ⓓ Ⓔ
14 Ⓐ Ⓑ Ⓒ Ⓓ Ⓔ	52 Ⓐ Ⓑ Ⓒ Ⓓ Ⓔ	90 Ⓐ Ⓑ Ⓒ Ⓓ Ⓔ
15 Ⓐ Ⓑ Ⓒ Ⓓ Ⓔ	53 Ⓐ Ⓑ Ⓒ Ⓓ Ⓔ	91 Ⓐ Ⓑ Ⓒ Ⓓ Ⓔ
16 Ⓐ Ⓑ Ⓒ Ⓓ Ⓔ	54 Ⓐ Ⓑ Ⓒ Ⓓ Ⓔ	92 Ⓐ Ⓑ Ⓒ Ⓓ Ⓔ
17 Ⓐ Ⓑ Ⓒ Ⓓ Ⓔ	55 Ⓐ Ⓑ Ⓒ Ⓓ Ⓔ	93 Ⓐ Ⓑ Ⓒ Ⓓ Ⓔ
18 Ⓐ Ⓑ Ⓒ Ⓓ Ⓔ	56 Ⓐ Ⓑ Ⓒ Ⓓ Ⓔ	94 Ⓐ Ⓑ Ⓒ Ⓓ Ⓔ
19 Ⓐ Ⓑ Ⓒ Ⓓ Ⓔ	57 Ⓐ Ⓑ Ⓒ Ⓓ Ⓔ	95 Ⓐ Ⓑ Ⓒ Ⓓ Ⓔ
20 Ⓐ Ⓑ Ⓒ Ⓓ Ⓔ	58 Ⓐ Ⓑ Ⓒ Ⓓ Ⓔ	96 Ⓐ Ⓑ Ⓒ Ⓓ Ⓔ
21 Ⓐ Ⓑ Ⓒ Ⓓ Ⓔ	59 Ⓐ Ⓑ Ⓒ Ⓓ Ⓔ	97 Ⓐ Ⓑ Ⓒ Ⓓ Ⓔ
22 Ⓐ Ⓑ Ⓒ Ⓓ Ⓔ	60 Ⓐ Ⓑ Ⓒ Ⓓ Ⓔ	98 Ⓐ Ⓑ Ⓒ Ⓓ Ⓔ
23 Ⓐ Ⓑ Ⓒ Ⓓ Ⓔ	61 Ⓐ Ⓑ Ⓒ Ⓓ Ⓔ	99 Ⓐ Ⓑ Ⓒ Ⓓ Ⓔ
24 Ⓐ Ⓑ Ⓒ Ⓓ Ⓔ	62 Ⓐ Ⓑ Ⓒ Ⓓ Ⓔ	100 Ⓐ Ⓑ Ⓒ Ⓓ Ⓔ
25 Ⓐ Ⓑ Ⓒ Ⓓ Ⓔ	63 Ⓐ Ⓑ Ⓒ Ⓓ Ⓔ	101 Ⓐ Ⓑ Ⓒ Ⓓ Ⓔ
26 Ⓐ Ⓑ Ⓒ Ⓓ Ⓔ	64 Ⓐ Ⓑ Ⓒ Ⓓ Ⓔ	102 Ⓐ Ⓑ Ⓒ Ⓓ Ⓔ
27 Ⓐ Ⓑ Ⓒ Ⓓ Ⓔ	65 Ⓐ Ⓑ Ⓒ Ⓓ Ⓔ	103 Ⓐ Ⓑ Ⓒ Ⓓ Ⓔ
28 Ⓐ Ⓑ Ⓒ Ⓓ Ⓔ	66 Ⓐ Ⓑ Ⓒ Ⓓ Ⓔ	104 Ⓐ Ⓑ Ⓒ Ⓓ Ⓔ
29 Ⓐ Ⓑ Ⓒ Ⓓ Ⓔ	67 Ⓐ Ⓑ Ⓒ Ⓓ Ⓔ	105 Ⓐ Ⓑ Ⓒ Ⓓ Ⓔ
30 Ⓐ Ⓑ Ⓒ Ⓓ Ⓔ	68 Ⓐ Ⓑ Ⓒ Ⓓ Ⓔ	106 Ⓐ Ⓑ Ⓒ Ⓓ Ⓔ
31 Ⓐ Ⓑ Ⓒ Ⓓ Ⓔ	69 Ⓐ Ⓑ Ⓒ Ⓓ Ⓔ	107 Ⓐ Ⓑ Ⓒ Ⓓ Ⓔ
32 Ⓐ Ⓑ Ⓒ Ⓓ Ⓔ	70 Ⓐ Ⓑ Ⓒ Ⓓ Ⓔ	108 Ⓐ Ⓑ Ⓒ Ⓓ Ⓔ
33 Ⓐ Ⓑ Ⓒ Ⓓ Ⓔ	71 Ⓐ Ⓑ Ⓒ Ⓓ Ⓔ	109 Ⓐ Ⓑ Ⓒ Ⓓ Ⓔ
34 Ⓐ Ⓑ Ⓒ Ⓓ Ⓔ	72 Ⓐ Ⓑ Ⓒ Ⓓ Ⓔ	110 Ⓐ Ⓑ Ⓒ Ⓓ Ⓔ
35 Ⓐ Ⓑ Ⓒ Ⓓ Ⓔ	73 Ⓐ Ⓑ Ⓒ Ⓓ Ⓔ	111 Ⓐ Ⓑ Ⓒ Ⓓ Ⓔ
36 Ⓐ Ⓑ Ⓒ Ⓓ Ⓔ	74 Ⓐ Ⓑ Ⓒ Ⓓ Ⓔ	112 Ⓐ Ⓑ Ⓒ Ⓓ Ⓔ
37 Ⓐ Ⓑ Ⓒ Ⓓ Ⓔ	75 Ⓐ Ⓑ Ⓒ Ⓓ Ⓔ	113 Ⓐ Ⓑ Ⓒ Ⓓ Ⓔ
38 Ⓐ Ⓑ Ⓒ Ⓓ Ⓔ	76 Ⓐ Ⓑ Ⓒ Ⓓ Ⓔ	114 Ⓐ Ⓑ Ⓒ Ⓓ Ⓔ

Item responses continued on reverse side.

SIDE 2

SUBJECT TEST

**COMPLETE THE
CERTIFICATION STATEMENT,
THEN TURN ANSWER SHEET
OVER TO SIDE 1.**

BE SURE EACH MARK IS DARK AND COMPLETELY FILLS THE INTENDED SPACE AS ILLUSTRATED HERE: ●.
YOU MAY FIND MORE RESPONSE SPACES THAN YOU NEED. IF SO, PLEASE LEAVE THEM BLANK.

115 Ⓐ Ⓑ Ⓒ Ⓓ Ⓔ	147 Ⓐ Ⓑ Ⓒ Ⓓ Ⓔ	179 Ⓐ Ⓑ Ⓒ Ⓓ Ⓔ	211 Ⓐ Ⓑ Ⓒ Ⓓ Ⓔ
116 Ⓐ Ⓑ Ⓒ Ⓓ Ⓔ	148 Ⓐ Ⓑ Ⓒ Ⓓ Ⓔ	180 Ⓐ Ⓑ Ⓒ Ⓓ Ⓔ	212 Ⓐ Ⓑ Ⓒ Ⓓ Ⓔ
117 Ⓐ Ⓑ Ⓒ Ⓓ Ⓔ	149 Ⓐ Ⓑ Ⓒ Ⓓ Ⓔ	181 Ⓐ Ⓑ Ⓒ Ⓓ Ⓔ	213 Ⓐ Ⓑ Ⓒ Ⓓ Ⓔ
118 Ⓐ Ⓑ Ⓒ Ⓓ Ⓔ	150 Ⓐ Ⓑ Ⓒ Ⓓ Ⓔ	182 Ⓐ Ⓑ Ⓒ Ⓓ Ⓔ	214 Ⓐ Ⓑ Ⓒ Ⓓ Ⓔ
119 Ⓐ Ⓑ Ⓒ Ⓓ Ⓔ	151 Ⓐ Ⓑ Ⓒ Ⓓ Ⓔ	183 Ⓐ Ⓑ Ⓒ Ⓓ Ⓔ	215 Ⓐ Ⓑ Ⓒ Ⓓ Ⓔ
120 Ⓐ Ⓑ Ⓒ Ⓓ Ⓔ	152 Ⓐ Ⓑ Ⓒ Ⓓ Ⓔ	184 Ⓐ Ⓑ Ⓒ Ⓓ Ⓔ	216 Ⓐ Ⓑ Ⓒ Ⓓ Ⓔ
121 Ⓐ Ⓑ Ⓒ Ⓓ Ⓔ	153 Ⓐ Ⓑ Ⓒ Ⓓ Ⓔ	185 Ⓐ Ⓑ Ⓒ Ⓓ Ⓔ	217 Ⓐ Ⓑ Ⓒ Ⓓ Ⓔ
122 Ⓐ Ⓑ Ⓒ Ⓓ Ⓔ	154 Ⓐ Ⓑ Ⓒ Ⓓ Ⓔ	186 Ⓐ Ⓑ Ⓒ Ⓓ Ⓔ	218 Ⓐ Ⓑ Ⓒ Ⓓ Ⓔ
123 Ⓐ Ⓑ Ⓒ Ⓓ Ⓔ	155 Ⓐ Ⓑ Ⓒ Ⓓ Ⓔ	187 Ⓐ Ⓑ Ⓒ Ⓓ Ⓔ	219 Ⓐ Ⓑ Ⓒ Ⓓ Ⓔ
124 Ⓐ Ⓑ Ⓒ Ⓓ Ⓔ	156 Ⓐ Ⓑ Ⓒ Ⓓ Ⓔ	188 Ⓐ Ⓑ Ⓒ Ⓓ Ⓔ	220 Ⓐ Ⓑ Ⓒ Ⓓ Ⓔ
125 Ⓐ Ⓑ Ⓒ Ⓓ Ⓔ	157 Ⓐ Ⓑ Ⓒ Ⓓ Ⓔ	189 Ⓐ Ⓑ Ⓒ Ⓓ Ⓔ	221 Ⓐ Ⓑ Ⓒ Ⓓ Ⓔ
126 Ⓐ Ⓑ Ⓒ Ⓓ Ⓔ	158 Ⓐ Ⓑ Ⓒ Ⓓ Ⓔ	190 Ⓐ Ⓑ Ⓒ Ⓓ Ⓔ	222 Ⓐ Ⓑ Ⓒ Ⓓ Ⓔ
127 Ⓐ Ⓑ Ⓒ Ⓓ Ⓔ	159 Ⓐ Ⓑ Ⓒ Ⓓ Ⓔ	191 Ⓐ Ⓑ Ⓒ Ⓓ Ⓔ	223 Ⓐ Ⓑ Ⓒ Ⓓ Ⓔ
128 Ⓐ Ⓑ Ⓒ Ⓓ Ⓔ	160 Ⓐ Ⓑ Ⓒ Ⓓ Ⓔ	192 Ⓐ Ⓑ Ⓒ Ⓓ Ⓔ	224 Ⓐ Ⓑ Ⓒ Ⓓ Ⓔ
129 Ⓐ Ⓑ Ⓒ Ⓓ Ⓔ	161 Ⓐ Ⓑ Ⓒ Ⓓ Ⓔ	193 Ⓐ Ⓑ Ⓒ Ⓓ Ⓔ	225 Ⓐ Ⓑ Ⓒ Ⓓ Ⓔ
130 Ⓐ Ⓑ Ⓒ Ⓓ Ⓔ	162 Ⓐ Ⓑ Ⓒ Ⓓ Ⓔ	194 Ⓐ Ⓑ Ⓒ Ⓓ Ⓔ	226 Ⓐ Ⓑ Ⓒ Ⓓ Ⓔ
131 Ⓐ Ⓑ Ⓒ Ⓓ Ⓔ	163 Ⓐ Ⓑ Ⓒ Ⓓ Ⓔ	195 Ⓐ Ⓑ Ⓒ Ⓓ Ⓔ	227 Ⓐ Ⓑ Ⓒ Ⓓ Ⓔ
132 Ⓐ Ⓑ Ⓒ Ⓓ Ⓔ	164 Ⓐ Ⓑ Ⓒ Ⓓ Ⓔ	196 Ⓐ Ⓑ Ⓒ Ⓓ Ⓔ	228 Ⓐ Ⓑ Ⓒ Ⓓ Ⓔ
133 Ⓐ Ⓑ Ⓒ Ⓓ Ⓔ	165 Ⓐ Ⓑ Ⓒ Ⓓ Ⓔ	197 Ⓐ Ⓑ Ⓒ Ⓓ Ⓔ	229 Ⓐ Ⓑ Ⓒ Ⓓ Ⓔ
134 Ⓐ Ⓑ Ⓒ Ⓓ Ⓔ	166 Ⓐ Ⓑ Ⓒ Ⓓ Ⓔ	198 Ⓐ Ⓑ Ⓒ Ⓓ Ⓔ	230 Ⓐ Ⓑ Ⓒ Ⓓ Ⓔ
135 Ⓐ Ⓑ Ⓒ Ⓓ Ⓔ	167 Ⓐ Ⓑ Ⓒ Ⓓ Ⓔ	199 Ⓐ Ⓑ Ⓒ Ⓓ Ⓔ	231 Ⓐ Ⓑ Ⓒ Ⓓ Ⓔ
136 Ⓐ Ⓑ Ⓒ Ⓓ Ⓔ	168 Ⓐ Ⓑ Ⓒ Ⓓ Ⓔ	200 Ⓐ Ⓑ Ⓒ Ⓓ Ⓔ	232 Ⓐ Ⓑ Ⓒ Ⓓ Ⓔ
137 Ⓐ Ⓑ Ⓒ Ⓓ Ⓔ	169 Ⓐ Ⓑ Ⓒ Ⓓ Ⓔ	201 Ⓐ Ⓑ Ⓒ Ⓓ Ⓔ	233 Ⓐ Ⓑ Ⓒ Ⓓ Ⓔ
138 Ⓐ Ⓑ Ⓒ Ⓓ Ⓔ	170 Ⓐ Ⓑ Ⓒ Ⓓ Ⓔ	202 Ⓐ Ⓑ Ⓒ Ⓓ Ⓔ	234 Ⓐ Ⓑ Ⓒ Ⓓ Ⓔ
139 Ⓐ Ⓑ Ⓒ Ⓓ Ⓔ	171 Ⓐ Ⓑ Ⓒ Ⓓ Ⓔ	203 Ⓐ Ⓑ Ⓒ Ⓓ Ⓔ	235 Ⓐ Ⓑ Ⓒ Ⓓ Ⓔ
140 Ⓐ Ⓑ Ⓒ Ⓓ Ⓔ	172 Ⓐ Ⓑ Ⓒ Ⓓ Ⓔ	204 Ⓐ Ⓑ Ⓒ Ⓓ Ⓔ	236 Ⓐ Ⓑ Ⓒ Ⓓ Ⓔ
141 Ⓐ Ⓑ Ⓒ Ⓓ Ⓔ	173 Ⓐ Ⓑ Ⓒ Ⓓ Ⓔ	205 Ⓐ Ⓑ Ⓒ Ⓓ Ⓔ	237 Ⓐ Ⓑ Ⓒ Ⓓ Ⓔ
142 Ⓐ Ⓑ Ⓒ Ⓓ Ⓔ	174 Ⓐ Ⓑ Ⓒ Ⓓ Ⓔ	206 Ⓐ Ⓑ Ⓒ Ⓓ Ⓔ	238 Ⓐ Ⓑ Ⓒ Ⓓ Ⓔ
143 Ⓐ Ⓑ Ⓒ Ⓓ Ⓔ	175 Ⓐ Ⓑ Ⓒ Ⓓ Ⓔ	207 Ⓐ Ⓑ Ⓒ Ⓓ Ⓔ	239 Ⓐ Ⓑ Ⓒ Ⓓ Ⓔ
144 Ⓐ Ⓑ Ⓒ Ⓓ Ⓔ	176 Ⓐ Ⓑ Ⓒ Ⓓ Ⓔ	208 Ⓐ Ⓑ Ⓒ Ⓓ Ⓔ	240 Ⓐ Ⓑ Ⓒ Ⓓ Ⓔ
145 Ⓐ Ⓑ Ⓒ Ⓓ Ⓔ	177 Ⓐ Ⓑ Ⓒ Ⓓ Ⓔ	209 Ⓐ Ⓑ Ⓒ Ⓓ Ⓔ	241 Ⓐ Ⓑ Ⓒ Ⓓ Ⓔ
146 Ⓐ Ⓑ Ⓒ Ⓓ Ⓔ	178 Ⓐ Ⓑ Ⓒ Ⓓ Ⓔ	210 Ⓐ Ⓑ Ⓒ Ⓓ Ⓔ	242 Ⓐ Ⓑ Ⓒ Ⓓ Ⓔ

IF YOU DO NOT WANT THIS ANSWER SHEET TO BE SCORED

If you want to cancel your scores from this administration, complete A and B below. You will not receive scores for this test; however, you will receive confirmation of this cancellation. No record of this test or the cancellation will be sent to the recipients you indicated, and there will be no scores for this test on your GRE file. Once a score is canceled, it cannot be reinstated.

To cancel your scores from this test administration, you must:

TR	TW	TFS	TCS	1R	1W	1FS	1CS	2R	2W	2FS	2CS
		FOR ETS USE ONLY		3R	3W	3FS	3CS	4R	4W	4FS	4CS
				5R	5W	5FS	5CS	6R	6W	6FS	6CS